from there to here

threads of deconstruction

Spiritual, Psychological, and Social Justice Reflections

Appalachian Southern Baptist through Vietnam War,
The Jesus People, to Buddhist Christian

Doug Henning, PhD

Print: 978-1-958670-55-2
Ebook: 978-1-958670-54-5

Printed in the United States of America

Library of Congress Cataloguing-in-Publication Data
From There to Here: Many Threads of Deconstruction, A Memoir of Spiritual, Psychological, Social Justice Reflections, Appalachian Southern Baptist through Vietnam, Jesus People, to Buddhist Christian / Doug Henning, PhD

dedication

To my wife Joyce, sons Scott and Matt,
and to my grandchildren Palin, Phoenix,
Penn, Zain, Noor, and Sami

Table of Contents

Preface

Parts of everyone's lives, are interesting to others. As a psychologist with 50 years of experience in counseling and therapy, I've found that many clients often express their appreciation for being listened to. At times, this has been the most critical aspect of their experience. Some pioneers in modern psychology and psychiatry have built entire theories of personality development and, therefore, therapeutic intervention, around the power of listening, being listened to, and reflecting on what they've heard their clients say. Most, if not all, contemporary approaches to psychotherapy include the importance of listening and being present in the moment. We gain a lot from being able to explain who we are and what we've experienced.

I've often said that I learned a lot, not just about the individual, but about the human experience by listening to my clients and students. I have always made notes about the session. Besides helping me remember what we talked about these notes help me evaluate both the client and my role as their therapist. The times I have felt I hadn't done an adequate job were when I didn't listen adequately and maybe even talked too much myself.

Listening to others' stories about their life events and journeys can not only inform us about others but also often deepen our understanding of ourselves. Further, our telling can serve as an encouragement for someone going through similar issues or as a caution to be wary of pitfalls or of making similar mistakes.

I enjoy reading and, now that I'm retired, often spend a couple of hours each day doing so. I particularly enjoy reading biographies and historical fiction that describe how people have lived. Now that I'm in the last chapter of my life, I've been thinking about purposefully passing some things on to my sons and grandchildren in hopes they might understand and perhaps even learn from what their father and grandfather has gone through. Or at least understand a little better what made the old man tick. As much as anything, I want my kids and grandkids to know how important it is—as my Grandfather Palin advised my dad when he married my mom to keep on keeping on, be like the old tree that keeps growing.

So, Scott, Matt and grandkids, remember, I'm writing this to you. Of course, if others want to eavesdrop, you're more than welcome to listen in.

It has often been said that children catch more from us as parents than we set out to teach them on purpose—more is caught than taught.

In teaching communication courses, I've stressed that non-verbal communication speaks louder than words. So, when non-verbal behaviors—such as facial expression, tone of voice, and body posture—do not match what is being said, it's the non-verbal cues that are believed. Included in the non-verbal portion is the degree of follow-through. For example, if we claim to be committed to being there for someone when they need us, but then routinely forget or let something else take priority, that speaks louder than our words. The verbal portion of communication is the proverbial tip of the communication iceberg.

This is not to say that words are meaningless. Words are necessary, but in and of themselves are often insufficient to convey one's message effectively, words provide clarification and added emphasis. When insufficient to convey a message, words provide clarification and added emphasis. Furthermore, when non-verbal and verbal communication convey two different messages, words are necessary to correct and clarify the miscommunication. Yet, the danger we see in Western societies is that we often put too much stock in what is spoken rather than in what the non-verbal speaks to us. Buddhism tells us that words often get in the way of knowing. Politicians serve as a great example of this problem.

I've said all of this as an introduction to my decision to write about some parts of my life that have been formative to my development, and may be of benefit to others on similar journeys and pilgrimages.

Metaphorically, I've thought of this journey as similar to crossing a mountain stream: wading in shallow and not-so-shallow rapids, stepping on large flat rocks, log jams, and small islands. Some islands, looked at first, like they were on the other side of the stream, only to find out the stream was actually going around the island. The stream on the back side of the island still begged to be crossed. Each one—large rock, island, log jam—that I've stopped on while crossing the stream or river, at least for a time, had a sense of reaching a destination from which to fish. (All stream anglers know that the best-looking holes, where the fish likely are, are always on the other side of the stream.) It was not uncommon to even fall in over my head with my fishing basket floating above me; other times, I'd stumble and bruise a knee. But these are just part of the experience of being on the stream.

Once, while fishing on Skate Creek, at the base of Mount Rainer, I was crossing the stream on a log jam several feet above some large boulders. I slipped on the wet moss, fell on my back, knocked the wind out of me, and broke a couple of ribs. Fortunately, I held on to my fly rod, which was my priority. Once I realized I could breathe, I did a quick inventory to see if I had broken anything else. I had gone downstream while my son Matt and my wife Joyce had gone upstream. I knew the noise of the rapids would make it impossible to be heard if I yelled. So I scooted the rest of the way across the log and gingerly worked my way down the bank to the edge of the stream. Then I propped myself up against a large rock and kept fishing. Steep embankments rose on either side of the stream. If I moved very much or tried to take a deep breath, the pain in my side was excruciating. I realized I couldn't climb out on my own. So I fished.

In some ways, this is how I've approached a lot of things in my life: Focus on what I know and avoid conflict, which can't be resolved at this

Fly fishing on mountain stream

time. Sometimes, at first blush, two concepts/perspectives seem true in and of themselves but appear to be in direct conflict with each other. However, with time and more information, they have turned out to be just different perspectives, two different ways of seeing the same thing. They really were not in conflict; they were just different, even complementary. Going fishing is sometimes the best thing to do when we can't do anything else.

Eventually, Joyce and Matt came along looking for me. They helped me up the steep bank through thick underbrush. One pulled on my better arm, and the other pushed from behind.

I always loved being by a mountain stream. It's felt like a time of rejuvenation for my soul. Even though I enjoyed catching mountain trout, the number of trout I caught was secondary to just being out there, usually with one or both of my sons and or with Joyce. Joyce didn't like fishing, so she would bring a book and sit on a rock or a log to read.

Doug and Matt on the Blue River in Colorado

Crossing the streams and rivers of life is like crossing those actual streams I described above. Many people I've known have remained in the same frames of mind their entire lives, even being second and third-generation democrats or republicans, Baptists, Jews, Muslims, and so on. That has not been the case for me. Staying the same actually feels like stagnation.

The Public Religion Research Institute reports that the percentage of Americans who say religion is the most important thing in their lives has continued to decline over the last few decades. Additionally, 24% of Americans report that they worship in a different faith tradition than they previously followed. This describes my journey. That said, even when I've made what others might see as dramatic ideological changes, I often find myself drawn back to a spiritual core.

As long as I can remember, I've been curious about how religious faith fits with science. And how the science of psychology fits and does not fit with religion and faith. At 7 years old in the early 1950s, on a visit my family made from Ashland, Kentucky, to Tacoma, Washington, was the first time I remember meeting my grandfather (Oscar) Henning. Somehow, I knew he was, or at least saw himself as the family patriarch. I don't remember the context of the conversation, but I asked him if it was possible that God used, or even created, the process of evolution in creating the world. His answer, as I recall it, was an emphatic NO. My dad was present, but I don't remember him saying a word. The message was obvious to me that those kinds of assertions and questions were not to be asked, and I learned to keep to myself.

So, all my life, I've understood evolution as a way the world creates and re-creates itself: deconstructs and reconstructs. It's how it maintains and balances itself. My Organismal Biology professor, in 1971, said the following in class one day: '*The accounts that various religions give of creation of the world are the writer's attempt to interpret God's attempt to explain a process that humans with limited knowledge cannot fully understand. Evolution, on the other hand, is humans' attempt to understand things they cannot fully understand either. The two do not conflict with each other. They're just different ways of looking at the same thing.* This was a tremendous insight for me and helped me relax and open my mind to finding the truth. It was an answer to my question at seven that I asked Grandpa Henning. When I was teaching, I used to tell students that all truth is God's truth, no matter where you find it: in church, or in the science lab, or in nature. *Different fingers pointing at the same thing, or at different parts of the same thing.*[1]

The transitions in perspectives you'll read about in my story have rarely been sudden; instead, they have taken place over several years or even a couple of decades. To expand on the river metaphor, the transitions are often similar to the confluence of two rivers or major streams. At first, the water can look tumultuous and tricky to navigate. But with time, the new river formed by the flowing of two waterways smooths out and becomes somewhat comfortable to swim and wade in.

---

1. Knitter, Paul & Haight, Roger (2015) *Jesus and Buddha,* Orbis Books

A caveat: What I have written speaks of me and no one else. Some frustrations I'll talk about are my own, and need not be understood as "shoulds" for others. Having said this, I hope that some of what I have said speaks to others and serves to either encourage them on their journey or to confirm that they are right where they should be—no change being desired or necessary. Ultimately, each of us must sort these things out for ourselves. As you read, you will discover I've added a fair amount of Buddhist thought to my Christianity. I've found that adding my increasing understanding of Buddhism to my faith has been a pleasing and satisfying alternative to throwing out my faith altogether.

introduction

Before the Beginning

Even though my earliest memories are of Ashland, Kentucky, in the late 1940s, my history really began a couple of generations before that. I didn't really get to know my grandparents until I was fourteen. However, these ancestors of mine clearly had an impact on me. They were people of powerful character, and I'd like to think I inherited some of their strengths. Both of my grandmothers lived to ripe old ages and remained cognitively alert. One died at 93 years of age; the other one lived to be 102.

My grandfather, Oscar Henning, left home in Minnesota at fourteen and wound up in Red Lodge, Montana, working as a cowboy in the late 1890s. Before I got back to Tacoma at fourteen, he apparently loved telling the other grandkids about his horse, Brownie, and the time he rode in a posse chasing bank robbers.(Joyce and I have driven through Red Lodge several times over the years. There is a historic brass plaque on an old bank building that says it was the site of a famous bank robbery. It's fun to think that that may be the one that my Grandpa has talked about.) Oscar met my grandmother, Letty, when she was traveling, passing through Red Lodge and Yellowstone on a thirteen-day stagecoach trip out to Washington. Oscar and Letty exchanged letters but met only seven times after that before they got married. They were married for more than sixty years.

Oscar and Letty had a bakery and doughnut company in Tacoma, and my dad and Uncle Bob delivered doughnuts to Tacoma restaurants. The Quality Doughnuts company lasted until the rise of labor unions, and the teamsters would not let Oscar employ his sons to drive the delivery truck. He then went to work in the shipyards. He was a blacksmith on the side. Behind his house, he had a shop that resembled a blacksmith's shop where he had worked as a young lad in Minot, North Dakota. His shop had a forge, an anvil, and various hammers and other tools. Each of the grandkids was given a hand forged hunting knife and a couple of kitchen knives made from Swedish Steel. According to Oscar, Swedish Steel was the best. I've already passed mine on to my two sons.

As with most grandmothers, Letty took charge of running the family. I remember Sunday dinners at her table of roast beef, beets from Oscar's garden, and unbelievably good gravy. They had a couple of cherry trees in their backyard. To prevent the birds from eating the cherries, Letty hung small pie tins from the tree branches and would occasionally go out and shoot rocks at the tins to scare off the birds. I was always impressed with how accurate she was. Letty always had a great sense of humor. I can never remember her being sad. Oscar died in his late eighties. Letty lived to be 102.

Letty lived on her own until she went into a nursing home at 102. She died a few months after that. She often said that her secret to a long, healthy life was eating at least one Russell Stover dark chocolate a day and eating bread made with refined flour. Whenever she would get a box of chocolates as a gift, if they were not Russell Stover, she would put them out on her kitchen table for visitors. She kept the Russell Stover Dark Chocolates hidden in her bedroom dresser. Even though I don't have the Russell Stover Chocolates, I often have a chocolate-covered caramel at night as dessert. I think Letty would approve.

My father, Donald, was their oldest son. When I was about nine or ten years old, on the way to church one Wednesday evening, he told me he needed to tell me something. He said that he had been married before he married my mother, Grace. He and his first wife, Ruth, had gotten married pretty young. They had a baby boy who died of crib death at only a few months old. Then Ruth died from acute leukemia a few months later. He met my mom at church, and they got married several years later. That was it. He never mentioned the baby or Ruth again. From time to time in our adult lives, my sisters and I would occasionally wonder out loud about Ruth. Then, a few years ago, when Joyce and I were going through some boxes of old pictures, we came across several profession-al-looking pencil drawings of fashion dresses and models, signed by Ruth Kohl. The drawings were quite good. So we did some digging into death records in Tacoma and found Ruth's death certificate, verified her maiden name, and found a niece of my father and Ruth's, Chelsa. Chelsa was still alive at 94 and living near her daughter, Cathy, in eastern Washington. So, on a road trip to Tacoma a year later, we stopped to meet Chelsa. Chelsa would be my cousin-of-sorts, along with her daughter, Cathy. The time with them was a real treat. I gained a couple of new cousins. Before we left to continue our trip to Tacoma, Cathy gave me an envelope containing Christmas Cards my dad had sent to Chelsa and her mother throughout the 1950s. The cards were of pictures of my sisters and me. So even though Ruth was never mentioned, my dad had kept in contact with her family, which we never knew existed. I've wondered if my mom knew he had stayed in contact with them.

The real takeaway from this discovery was the revelation of my dad's young adult life after high school, which he never talked about. By Chelsa's report, my dad and Ruth were childhood sweethearts. He de-livered doughnuts to Ruth's parents' corner store. I can only imagine the heartache my dad went through in his early twenties, losing a baby and then his wife. He also essentially lost Ruth's family by eventually losing touch with them. It is sad to me that he never felt okay talking about any of that with my sisters or me. He actually only mentioned Ruth when he got dementia in his mid-eighties. I imagine the dementia resulted in him not being able to suppress those memories any longer. He would get confused about who he knew and the names of his kids, and would talk about his wife, Ruth.

My other grandmother, Harriet Palin, was a true adventurer and sur-vivor of the highest order. Harriet's husband was my mom's stepfather,

Willard. Harriet was a strong woman, and Willard was the epitome of a self-made man. Willard discovered a way to re-refine used motor oil in his basement. He got a tank truck and charged gas stations and mechanic shops to haul away their used, dirty motor oil. He then would re-refine it and sell it back to the same mechanics. From this, he also developed a way of making oil-based paint and built a paint factory. He made a lot of money before Congress passed the income tax in 1909 and ratified it in 1913 in the 16th Amendment. As the story goes, he was a shrewd entrepreneur in Tacoma. Yet the vivid memory I have of him is when we traveled out to Tacoma from Ashland, Kentucky when I was nearly eight years old in1953. We were in downtown Tacoma getting ready to cross the street. He insisted on holding my hand, probably thinking I wouldn't have had experience crossing busy intersections in Ashland like the ones that were in Tacoma. A panhandler was sitting on the corner with an open box, hoping for money. Grandpa (Willard) Palin put some money in the box. One of my parents asked him why he did that. Didn't he think the guy would spend it on alcohol? His answer: *I don't know how he will spend it. But I'd rather give some money, even at the risk of the person wasting it, than risk not giving it to someone who really needed it.* That was well over 70 years ago. I've never forgotten that. This is a thread that would endure throughout my life. Willard died of cancer in 1959, just a few days before we arrived back in Tacoma when we moved from Ashland. Not knowing him better is a genuine regret of mine.

Evidence that Harriet was a survivor: First, she survived a divorce in the 1930s when she was a member of the First Baptist Church of Tacoma (think conservative Christians of the first order). Then she married a divorced man she knew in her church. Second, she survived a radical double mastectomy for breast cancer in the mid-twentieth century. Following Willard's death in 1959, she continued to run the paint factory they had built for several more years. She and Willard had always talked about traveling the world when they retired, but never did it because they were running and managing the factory. Grandma eventually decided to sell the factory and travel on her own—by herself. She would take four and five-month-long trips on ocean freighters around the world. She lost track of how many around-the-world trips she took over the course of her lifetime. She preferred freighters because they only had a few passengers—10-12; and they always put into ports where ocean liners would never go. She often took these cruises during the winter holidays because she didn't want to be home without Willard at that time of year. As a teenager, I loved it when she would return from her trips. She always had great stories and unique gifts for us from all over the world. On one cruise, when going through the Straits of Magellan at the tip of South America, the pilot who was supposed to guide the ship through the straits turned out to be drunk. Getting too close to some islands, he ran the freighter aground. The ship began to sink in the middle of the night and rolled onto its side. So she, along with the other passengers and crew members, had to climb down rope ladders into lifeboats to make it to land. Her biggest regret was that she had been carrying an urn with Willard's ashes on all of her trips so she could spread some ashes around various parts of the world. The urn went down with the ship and was not recovered.

On another trip, the freighter had put into a port in the Philippine, Islands. She was in a taxi carrying several other people, one of whom was a son or nephew of a high-ranking government official. When they were traveling through some mountain passes some would-be assassins ambushed and attacked the taxi. The taxi driver was shot in the neck, which was not fatal, but he bled pretty badly. He kept driving as fast as he could. Grandma was sitting behind him, taking out her handkerchief, reaching over the seat, and holding it over the wound while he drove quickly through the mountains to get away from the assassins. This Story made the Manila news. Harriet Palin, well over sixty years of age, was a true adventurer and a real inspiration to Joyce and me as we've traveled over the last forty years. Don't wait, do it now!

PART 1

Low SATs, Vietnam, Jesus People,
grad school, college teaching,
Buddha & growing faith.

A Personal Memoir

chapter 1 - first thread

Appalachia Southern Baptist

I spent my boyhood in Eastern Kentucky on the edge of Appalachia in the late 1940s and 1950s. My father was a Chiropractor. When I was a toddler, we moved to Kentucky after my dad graduated from Chiropractic College in Indianapolis, Indiana. We were a deeply religious Southern Baptist family. Knowing what I know now, seven decades later, I have wondered if we might have been only a few hollows/hollers[1] from snake handlers deeper in Appalachia. I distinctly remember sitting on our front porch, looking on with interest across our country road into a pasture where Pentecostal revivalists had rented and pitched their tents. They were singing loud, energetic songs, hollering and carrying on. My dad inferred they were 'not quite right' and obviously not really as good Christians as we were because they were so apparently out of control and not at all like Baptists conducted themselves—as real Christians should.

My father was gifted with a delightful tenor singing voice, and as such was always the song leader and choir director as well as a soloist in the churches we attended. In fact, in the tri-state area of Eastern Kentucky, West Virginia, and Ohio, he was very often the featured "music

---

1. *Hollow, or Holler, in Southeast U.S. is a small valley between mountains*

evangelist" for revival meetings at other churches. Southern Baptists held revival meetings in the spring and fall.[2] I remember seeing his picture on posters in small grocery stores, inviting people to attend the meetings.

We were quite literally in church every time the doors opened. My sisters often fell asleep on and under the church pews. To say the least, my father was serious and earnest churchman. I was seven and eight years older than my sisters, Dawn and Noel. Sometimes, when my dad was doing a revival I would ride along with him through the rolling hills of tobacco farms and small towns. One particular church I have memories of was in Rose Hill, Kentucky. The evangelist was a large man, a recovered alcoholic, and a converted carnival wrestler. He was the stereotypical fire-and-brimstone preacher. At nine or ten years old, I was pretty taken with this guy. I remember him getting after some high school boys in the balcony who were chewing tobacco and sitting with their feet on the railing. You had the idea that if they didn't settle down, he was going to go up there and throw them out on their ears.

As long as I can remember, I've had a sensitivity to spiritual things. Whether this is because of my very early indoctrination to religious thinking or a natural leaning toward things spiritual, I can't tell. One could argue that spiritual sensitivities are inherent in our genes. My grandmother's brother, Uncle Charlie, was a mystic. He had a crystal ball and would read palms. He was also a railroad man and was on the run between Brainard, Minnesota, and Tacoma, Washington. There were stories of him stopping in little towns to gaze into his crystal ball and tell people their future, as well as prescribe some magical cure for an illness. My grandfather, Oscar, also read palms, but not always accurately. He had told my wife Joyce that she would have a hard, complicated pregnancy and have problems with the delivery of our first son. I was in Thailand helping fight the Vietnam War when he told her this. Her pregnancy and delivery were thankfully relatively easy, as pregnancies go. My grandmother said Joyce was built to have babies, like shelling peas. Grandpa predicted my youngest sister's divorce. Divorce rates of marriages that occurred under the age of twenty

---

2. *Even at a young age I thought of a "revival" as being a more spontaneous occurrence rather than a planned even. The idea of scheduling a revival for a particular week in the Spring and Fall a year or so ahead of time seem incongruent to me.*

turned out to be close to eighty percent. So really, it didn't take a lot of talent to predict.

Because we were always in church, it was the source of our social and cultural lives. Sunday School and Training Union (the Southern Baptist version of Sunday evening Sunday school), is where we were taught bible stories and life lessons. These were the sources of our indoctrination. As kids, we learned the Bible forward and backward. We took part in Sword Drills, the Bible being the Sword of the Lord. These took place throughout the year, getting ready for contests with other church youth groups at summer camps and district assemblies. Sword Drills were contests to see who could find a scriptural text the fastest. In the summers, we went to church camps and attended Daily Vacation Bible School. When we got older, we helped teach the younger ones.

My dad was apparently a good Chiropractor, but he was not a great businessman. So his practice often had people owing him more than he ever really collected. Although the business side of his Chiropractic practice was not a booming success financially, he was well-liked and respected in the town of Ashland. He was president of the local Optimist Club and a featured tenor in the Ashland Male Chorus. We lived above my dad's office in an old three-story house half a block from Main Street and across the alley from the back of Sears and Roebuck.

This location allowed me to get quite an education. I was impressed with a one-armed junk truck driver who picked up trash driving a large, rusted, old flat-bed truck with plywood sides that flopped to the side if not tied up with ropes. His one arm was amputated at the elbow. He could back his old truck into a narrow loading dock at the back of Sears with the stub of his amputated arm placed in a leather socket strapped to the steering wheel. Other drivers backed their tractor-trailer rigs into the same loading dock of Sears and other stores whose back docks were distributed along the ally—A & P Grocery, Woolworth's Five and Dime— but no one made such an impression as the one-armed man. I can still see this man in my memory in his dirty bib overalls with a cigarette hanging from his mouth. As I've thought about it since then, he probably looked like a typical hillbilly. All truck drivers smoked and always had a cigarette hanging out of their mouths. When they were finished with their smokes, they would throw the butts on the ground. Bums and hobos would walk through the alleyways and pick up the butts so they could light them again—free smokes.

At six and seven years old, I was fascinated with the men who picked up cigarette butts and re-lit them. So, naturally, my friends and I tried it. I'm sure we were convinced that this meant we were tough. I don't imagine that we inhaled, sort of like President Bill Clinton's claim that he never inhaled pot in college. We played hide and seek, kick-the-can in the alleyways, tried to smoke cigarette butts, watched bums drink Aqua Velva aftershave for cheap alcohol that they had bought from a barbershop, and watched the bats swoop down between the buildings at dusk. I remember my friend Dan's mom sitting on the back porch of their house, which backed up to the alley, cleaning catfish, smoking a cigarette, eating a sandwich, and drinking a beer.

This was segregated Eastern Kentucky in the 1950s. There was a Colored Town, literally on the other side of the tracks, close to the banks of the Ohio River. This was before flood walls, and was the area that always flooded when the Ohio River overflowed its banks. My dad would say he didn't understand why those people kept rebuilding there when they knew the Ohio would overflow again in a year or two. Apparently, my dad never realized that this was because of segregation, as well as it being the only part of town they were allowed to live in and could afford to live in. It was only on very rare occasions that I saw a black person, except for picking up trash in the alleys. The prevailing opinion was that Coloreds weren't very intelligent, so it was good that they could collect trash and, I suppose, get paid somehow for doing it. I imagine they would also use the cardboard and tin to make repairs on their houses down by the river.

This is a good example of how a foundation of prejudice gets interwoven into a culture and perpetuates racism. The prejudice is reinforced in self-perpetuating cycles. It was probably true that Black people didn't do as well on tasks that required more sophisticated and learned cognitive skills. But this was because of the lower quality of education, outdated textbooks, larger class sizes, lower expectations from society, and a higher dropout rate than their white counterparts.

Later, when I was in the eighth grade, we moved to Tacoma, Washington. For the first time, I went to school with Black kids.

When I was about eight, we moved from the house across the alley-way behind Sears and Roebuck to the country. We had a couple of acres: a chicken coup, a pretty large chicken yard, and a sizeable garden. This is where I began learning more about being a hillbilly. Education did not matter all that much in Kentucky. My dad used to joke that we were thankful for Mississippi because it was 48th out of the then 48 states in education—Kentucky was 47th. My friends' dads from school and church either worked at the local steel mill or Ashland Oil.

My friends and I slept out in the backyard in the summer and scared each other with ghost stories of tales of crazy people that had escaped from a mental hospital. We had lots of tall pine trees on our property, which, in the middle of the night, with the moon shining through the branches, cast scary shadows. I would have gone into the house to be safe, but I was afraid that if I moved, whatever monster or ghost was in the trees would get me. So I prayed that I'd still be alive in the morning. My new friends and I played in the woods and naturally got into some mischief from time to time. We'd chase and were chased by the neighbor's cows and donkeys, scare ours and the neighbor's chickens.

I liked to go into the chicken coop with a rainbow-colored umbrella. I'd spin the umbrella in front of the chickens, who were on the roost, and some would get dizzy and have a hard time hanging on to the roost. When my dad found this out, he blamed me for the drop in egg produc-tion. We had about 15 laying hens and always had a bunch of setters. The result being lots of young roosters by the end of summer. So, on a particular Saturday in the fall, my dad and I would slaughter the roosters by cutting off their heads and letting them flop around. I had watched my friend's mother, Mrs. Johnson, kill her friers by wringing their necks with one hand. She would hold the chicken's head in the palm of her hand and make a jerking motion, snapping its neck. This really impressed me, and at ten years old, I thought I could probably do that. I was obviously not strong enough, and at ten, I certainly didn't have the technique down. All I really did was make the poor young roosters a little dizzy before chop-ping off its head with the hatchet.

I had a few chores. I mowed the lawn throughout the spring and summer, weeded the garden, which I hated, and cleaned the chicken coup. I hated cleaning the chicken coop even more. I was supposed to clean it every month and spread the manure in the garden. But I often "forgot," so the manure would just pile up. Since the coup was closed in, the smell was awful when I would begin digging through the manure with a pitchfork to put it in the wheelbarrow. The pungent smell of composting chicken manure was enough to make my stomach do flips. The longer I put off cleaning the coop, the worse it got.

I'm sure there is a life lesson in there. Problems are usually best dealt with sooner rather than later. The longer we put off dealing with issues, the worse they smell, and the more complex the solution is and takes longer.

Another interesting characteristic of chicken coups: chicken feed is poured into hanging feeders suspended just above the floor from the ceiling. So the chickens could stand on the floor and peck at the feed. Sometimes, when opening the door to the coop, the hanging feeder would be swinging without chickens standing close. Occasionally, if I approached the coop very quietly, I could surprise the rat (- or often rats) on the feeder before they jumped off. Although we had a couple of cats, they were only mousers. They apparently didn't do rats. This was probably because the rats were as big as the cats. Then, rather suddenly, we stopped seeing the rats. One weekend morning, when I was straightening up the coop, I moved a bale of straw we used for bedding in the egg nests. There was a copperhead snake. It apparently had gotten rid of the rats for us.

Living in the country in the foothills of the Appalachian Mountains, I had contact with real country hillbillies. Many of my friends had outhouses behind their houses and Sears catalogs for toilet paper. Most of them had only cold running water in their houses. Our house had hot and cold running water in the kitchen and bathroom. The bathroom jutted out from the back of the house, where it had been added on. I was introduced to serious smoking, drinking hootch/moonshine, and pornography of the mid-1950s.

Since I was a good aspiring Southern Baptist, I was afraid to try drinking alcohol. This came under the heading of things you did not want to be doing when the Lord came back—when the rapture happened. The list of things not to be doing when the Lord returned was rather long. This was the church of don'ts: don't go to school dances, play pool in the bowling alley, curse, or play pinball machines. Pinball was like gambling, because you could win free games. Neither could we play cards if we used a poker deck—not even fish or hearts. It was, however, ok to make our own cards and put numbers on them, which we did.

However, smoking tobacco was a different story. This was Kentucky in the 1950s, after all. One of the major agricultural products was to-bacco. Therefore, a significant portion of Sunday collection-plate income came directly or indirectly from the tobacco industry. It seemed like all adults smoked. Even on Sunday, there was a fifteen-minute break be-tween Sunday School and the preaching service. This was so the men could stand on the front porch and smoke two cigarettes—seven minutes each. Mom smoked but thought she hid it from us. My dad smoked a pipe, saying that it was not as harmful to his singing voice as cigarettes were. My dad had asthma, so he always carried his spray[3] with him. As a kid, I never made the connection that his smoking may have been the reason his asthma would often flare up. Later in his life, he switched to chewing cigars and did so until he went into a nursing home at eighty-three. I tried learning to smoke but never really got the hang of it. In the military, I occasionally smoked a cigar. I guess I thought it just came with the territory and made me tough. The cigars often just flared up my asthma, too.

I don't remember if the move to the country was stressful for me. The things I remember most are that my fourth-grade teacher would smack kids' palms with a long ruler when we weren't paying attention or some other serious infraction, the school was K-12. When I was in fifth grade, the district built an elementary school across a dirt road that ran beside our house.

In fifth grade, much to my embarrassment, I began to develop a stut-ter. Looking back, this may have been due to the stress of the move and the need to make new friends. The stutter became quite pronounced when

---

3. *An atomizer with liquid medicine. This was before packaged inhalers.*

I was nervous. In sixth grade, the teacher would call on us to stand by our desks and read out loud from a textbook. As I would stutter my way through the passage I was attempting to read, some kids would laugh. I suppose it was pretty funny, at least to them. The teacher didn't tell them to stop. Her approach was to tell me to read slower and think about what I was going to say. My parents used the same approach. All it did was make the stutter worse. I could feel my face turn red with embarrassment and frustration.

Early in my psychology training, I learned that focusing on the thing and worrying about what you don't want to do usually only serves to reinforce the behavior, making it worse and strengthening the undesirable behavior. Thinking about what one doesn't want to do keeps the behavior in the forefront of our thinking, and the behavior most often gets worse. Thus, the solution, to the extent you are able, is to look at it as a "So What". It is what it is. The behavior is already a part of who you are. By accepting it as just the way things are, we take away the behavior's emotional power. Fear and guilt have a way of keeping things we dread in the forefront of our thoughts, so that anytime there is a pause in our thinking, that's what we think about, which is a form of reinforcement. So believing that a part of us is awful, awful-izing it, we actually make the habit stronger. So the paradoxical goal is to embrace it, accept it as just being a part of who we are. Embracing it is the first step toward taking control of what feels out of control. This way, it is no longer at the forefront of our thinking, just like not obsessing over what color our eyes are.[4] This may be what Apostle Paul was getting at when he said that he "rejoices in his weakness so that the power of Christ is made perfect in him"

RC COLA (Royal Crown Cola)

Across the road from my house was a large gravel turnaround for the city bus from Ashland. We were at the end of the line. On the edge of the turnaround was a little country store, Ashby's Store. Think of a scene from The

---

4. Psychologically, this approach is part of Cognitive Behavior and Gestalt Therapy known as *paradoxical intent (PI)*. This therapeutic technique was developed by Victor Frankel an Austrian Psychiatrist and Holocaust survivor. By doing, or at least allowing the behavior to exist, the undesirable behavior or thought processes begins to weaken, paradoxically, under the control of the person.

Andy Griffith Show. This was straight out of Mayberry. When you entered the store, a bell attached to the door would ring. The floor was uneven, with wood planks that creaked, and there were wooden-framed glass-covered counters between you and the items on the shelves. The counters were arranged in a U shape, with merchandise on shelves behind them. Upon hearing the bell ring, Mr. or Mrs. Ashby would emerge through a curtain hanging in a doorway. (They lived in the back of the store.) They would stand behind the counter, ready to get what you wanted. There was also a cold-soda-pop chest by the door filled with bottles of RC Cola, Pepsi, Coke, NEHI Orange and Grape soda, and, of course, Hires Root Beer. A bottle of pop was a nickel. After doing our chores or after a game of baseball or football in Mrs. Johnson's cow pasture, we would often gather at Ashby's store. So, a familiar scene was when a few of my friends and I were sitting on the porch of the store, drinking an RC, into which we poured a small bag of Planters Peanuts and ate a Moon Pie. The peanuts would float, so you could eat them as you drank the RC.

Most of my friends had nicknames. My best friends were Frog (Larry), Frog's big brother Bubby (Donavan), Buddy (Perry), and June Bug (Junior). Not sure why I didn't have a nickname. If I had, it might have been Tubby. So it's just as well I didn't have one. My mother would have absolutely NOT approved of that name for me. Any time someone referred to my physique as heavy, or some other negative term for fat, she would quickly correct them, saying I was "husky."

One bit of contraband that I discovered while living in the country in Kentucky was illegal fireworks. Fireworks, besides sparklers, were illegal in Boyd County. But my friends and their older brothers had "connections" to sources across the state line in West Virginia. So I could buy them from these older boys. Since I had to pay for them, I figured I could make a little money by running firecrackers to my friends at church for a little bit of profit, of course. My friends' dads were deacons or Sunday school teachers and, of course, the pastor's son. I don't remember exactly how long I was able to hide this business from my parents. But one Sunday afternoon, when we got home, my dad approached me, saying that one of my friends had ratted on me, saying the source of his fireworks was me. It may well have been that one of my friends was supplying his friends in school. Even though the firecracker business came to an abrupt end, it turned out to be the impetus for other entrepreneurial ventures.

I built a wagon that hooked to my bike to carry our power lawn mower. This way, I could haul it to various lawn jobs I had. In late summer, I also carried paper bags of apples from our several apple trees and sold them to small country stores along the way. I also made pot-holders with a loom I had made and sold them door to door. Sales came relatively easily for me. Looking back, this may have been in part because of my stutter. While this was a source of terrible embarrassment to me in school, it may have endeared me to moms who came to the door when I was peddling my wares. In the cute department, being chubby and having curly hair probably didn't hurt, either.

I also used to ask if I could have various old bicycles that were in obvious disrepair and lying in the yard. I'd haul them home in the trailer behind my bike. I figured I could take the parts from several bikes, make a few working bikes, and then sell them. I'm sure I gave away one or two working bikes and kept two cooler bikes for myself. I don't remember if I ever actually sold a working parts bike. My mom told me she was afraid that having rusty bikes in the backyard would morph into rusty cars in the yard, which was not uncommon in the country where we lived.

The last business venture I attempted was the most enterprising. At least I thought so. I was sure it was a «no-lose." Somehow, I had seen a mail flyer that advertised a money maker for organizations like church choirs, Cub Scouts, and the like. You only had to buy 144 coffee-sized canisters of *Mrs Leland's Old Fashioned Golden Butter Bits* for $90.00. Each can sold for one dollar. So it was clear, at twelve years old, what an opportunity this was. I ordered one gross, 144 cans. I had failed to tell my parents of my venture. I had put my dad's office address on the order form. So one day, several boxes, a 'gross' probably in more ways than one, of golden butter bits, were delivered to my dad's office. I had three months to pay the bill. My dad and mom were surprised but not impressed. But I was confident. The first twenty-five went like hotcakes—family, friends, and choir members at church. The pace slowed down some, but I was not to be deterred. Then, the pace of sales slowed significantly. What I had failed to consider was the fact that I was not the only one in the area who had seen the advertisement. Several organizations started selling the golden butter bits. The market was flooded. I did finally sell enough to pay the $90.00, with a little help from my parents. More on the butter bits business in a minute.

Since the business part of my dad's Chiropractic practice was essentially a failure, when my grandfather, my mom's stepfather, Grandpa Palin, had terminal cancer and was soon to die, the decision to move back to Tacoma was, by all intents and purposes, fairly easy. I was fourteen, and my sisters were six and seven. As I remember this time, I don't recall ever talking about moving. The decision was just announced.

chapter 2

Moving to Washington Thread

We sold the house lock, stock, and barrel—all the furniture, lawn mower, lawn tools, and bicycles went with it. My dad sold his practice. We bought a new 1959 Chevy station wagon and a Shasta travel trailer and left town. It took us seven days to make the trip from Ashland to Tacoma, Washington.

At this point, I still had fifty cans of Butter Bits. So, along the way, when we would stop at a camping spot for the night, my parents *encouraged* me to go around to other campers and try to sell my wares. I sold a few cans by the time we landed in Tacoma. But I had a new territory to try. With encouragement from my parents again, I was able to sell several more. But certainly not all forty-plus cans.

For the next few years, relatives would receive a can of Butter Bits for Christmas. This became a family joke for years to come.

As an aside, my brother-in-law's family was going through their attic several years ago and came across an empty can of the Butter Bits. (A selling point of the candy was that it came in a decorative can with a decorative plastic lid to be used as a kitchen canister.) Terry, had lived about a half mile from where we lived. Their house was on my way to school. Apparently, I had sold the can to his mom. An additional funny thing is that Terry's family owned a corner drugstore that specialized in a soda fountain and a candy shop. Terry and my sister, Noel, didn't meet until several decades later.

We moved to Tacoma during the summer of 1959. Interestingly, I don't remember thinking much about it; the move just happened. As I mentioned earlier, Kentucky schools were among the worst in the country, and Washington schools were rated at the top. Thus, starting eighth grade in Washington, I was way behind. I was in bonehead math and English classes. Looking back, I never really caught up academically until my late 20s after I got out of the Air Force during the Vietnam War. Fortunately, my sisters, since they were in the first years of elementary school, seemed able to catch up academically.

Because the laws governing the practice of Chiropractic in Washington were stricter than in Kentucky, my dad decided not to continue with his Chiropractic profession. (I think he was afraid he wouldn't be able to pass the licensing exam after being out of school for several years.) Through a Christian Men's organization, he was offered a sales job in a high-end furniture store. But he didn't take it because he didn't want to punch a clock. So he got a series of other jobs: a masseuse in an exercise center, and then opening his own Swedish Massage clinic. Later, as those jobs didn't work out, he got a job selling church pews to churches building new buildings or upgrading their interiors. This put him in direct contact with churches, which he saw as a "ministry" of sorts. He really liked this aspect of the job. I've often thought that he would have been happier when he was deciding what he wanted to be, if he had gone to seminary and focused on music.

Looking back, my mom was always the one who seemed more responsible when it came to work and earning an income. She always had a secretarial or bookkeeping job and, on weekends, would work other jobs: waiting tables for a local catering company, restaurant work at the state fair in the fall, and handing out food samples at supermarkets. Although, my dad's lack of motivation to work at the best job he could get seemed to be a source of conflict for them, they prided themselves on never having an argument or fighting. But there were times when they didn't speak to each other for a few days at a time. My dad would be gone earlier in the morning than he needed to actually leave and stay up late into the night after mom had gone to bed.

Upon our arrival in Tacoma, Dad quickly found a Southern Baptist Church that needed a minister of music. (Being the minister of music in relatively small churches probably never paid much, if anything.) But we had a new church home where my sisters and I continued, without missing a step, with our indoctrination and learning to get ready to live the lives of good Southern Baptist Christians. We received pins for perfect attendance to wear on our Sunday clothes, we found girlfriends and boyfriends at church and at summer camps, and most importantly, we learned how to speak the language of Conservative Evangelical Christianity. I learned to *believe what I was supposed to believe.*

I sort of recovered socially from the drastic move at fourteen and had a few good friends by the time I was in High School. Although I missed my friends in Kentucky, I never communicated with them. Just five or six years ago, I got a message on Facebook asking me if I was the Doug Henning who used to live in Ashland, Kentucky. It was from Roger, who had been one of my best friends. He said that he was glad to find me and to know what had happened to me. He had come back from visiting his grandparents in Ohio the summer we moved, and I was gone. Someone had bought our house and was living in it. We communicated back and forth a few times to learn what we had been up to, had been caught up in the Vietnam War?, and that was that.

The most stressful part of the move to Washington had to do with a much higher-quality public education system. Besides being overweight and relatively shy, I was embarrassed at being in bonehead math and English classes. By the time I was in high school, my stutter was pretty bad. Unusual for the time (early 60s), and before the time of special education, the Tacoma school district provided speech therapy in the school for students who had speech impediments. So, twice a week, two other boys and I went to speech therapy. The therapist's name was Mr. Ravey if I remember correctly. I credit him with helping me cope more effectively with my stutter.

Even now I still have a tendency to stutter when I get a little nervous, like when meeting new people. But thanks to Mr. Ravey, I hide my stutter pretty well with a slight pause today. Even though my stutter was better controlled, it was still present; I had just learned to pause briefly for certain words or substitute easier words. Most people, besides Joyce and close family members, think I'm thinking or pausing for effect. Some words are more likely to trigger a stutter. Words beginning with a heavy 'P' sound are the worst. I used to joke that living in the Puget Sound region in Pierce County, Tacoma, attending Pacific Lutheran University, working for a while at People's Church, and living in Puyallup for the last 20 years we lived in Washington all made it tricky when introducing myself. Fortunately, my profession, Psychology, does not have that heavy 'P' sound.

A positive aspect of moving to Tacoma was getting to know my grandparents, aunts, uncles, and cousins. We had met them once or twice on trips from Ashland. So, I gained a larger family. Danny was my Aunt Dorthy's son, my mom's sister's son. Danny went to the junior high school and the senior high school, where I would attend. So, I had a friend right off the bat. My other cousins were my dad's brother's family, Uncle Bob and Aunt Iris, and four cousins. I really thought they were cool. They lived in Puyallup, eight miles from Tacoma. They were all very musical and played a variety of instruments. My cousin Tag would eventually play in a popular rock and roll band in the Pacific Northwest, Mary Lee Rush and the Turnabouts. Tag had a reputation as one of the best base players in the northwest. Brad would become a leader of a weekly religious meeting in the 60s and 70s, *Saturday Night Meeting*, composed of college students and Jesus People. This meeting lasted for over a decade, until the early 80s. Laurel was a year older than I was. She would occasionally bail me out and be my date when I needed a date but was too shy to ask someone else. Laurel passed away in the Fall of 2023 from Acute Leukemia. Even though we didn't see each other very often because we moved from Puyallup thirty-plus years ago when we moved to Kansas for me to teach college, I miss her more than I anticipated. Carolyn, the oldest of my cousins and an anthropologist, has been a friend and an academic role model for me—is an author and researcher. and a college professor. Their family always seemed to have a lot of fun together, more than my family did. Because I thought they were cool, I always cared about what I imagined their opinions were of me. I remember the sadness and tears when I heard Uncle Bob had passed away after a battle with misdiagnosed cancer. It was February 1970. We were living in Minot, North Dakota, by then, where I was finishing out my four years in the Air Force after my time in Thailand during the Vietnam War.

In the early 60s, church life and summer church camps made up for the gaps socially. I had learned the Conservative Christian language so well that I appeared to others, as well as myself, to be a mature young Christian. At eighteen, I was elected to the church board of deacons. This was before I went off to college in Portland, Oregon. And *I really believed* what I thought I believed. I've often thought that being on the board of deacons at eighteen must have made my parents proud and probably helped my self-image; it was actually a terrible thing to do to a kid. A couple of smart sociologists once said, "Nothing is more dangerous than the truth thought found" and "Nothing is more tragic than success found too early." I was in for some surprises, for sure.

I took the SATs at the beginning of my senior year in high school. They were truly awful: somewhere in the 200s, if I remember correctly. I sat across from the high school counselor to review my results and think about a plan for my future. I still remember the feeling of having cold water thrown in my face. He said it was no wonder I had flunked Spanish. According to my scores, I could barely speak English. I must have asked something about which college he recommended. He said I should forget college altogether and think about attending a relatively easy local trade school. But I was not to be deterred. When spring semester came around, I took the advice of an older friend at church who was home from college. He liked the small college he was attending in Portland, Oregon. So, I applied to Cascade College.

My type of denial is a common human tendency and can actually serve us well. Failing to realistically and objectively see one's true ability to accomplish or chances of success at a task enables people to hang in there even when the odds are against them. So, somewhere along the line, I had gained this sense of self-efficacy, even though there was little objective data to support it. Truth be known, being a small Christian college, Cascade was heavily tuition-dependent. So I think they accepted just about anyone, knowing that many of those who got accepted would probably not be around by the end of their first or second year. Good, that I didn't know that. I had been accepted and was going to be a college student.

PART 2

chapter 3

College Thread

COLLEGE I

Cascade was a small (450 students) conservative Christian college. Fortunately, it was not a Southern Baptist college, which forced me to begin looking at things from a slightly different perspective. It was associated with the Wesleyan doctrine: Evangelical United Brethren [EUB], Nazarene, Methodist. This was the first time I was around students and faculty who had different beliefs/doctrines and languages than I was used to. I actually handled this pretty well. Their views on baptism, salvation, and related matters, although they seemed like a big deal, were interesting to me and made sense. Adding these different perspectives to my Sunday School like faith happened pretty smoothly, at least with hindsight. Even in my late teens, I was open to new ways of thinking. To add new ways of thinking and believing, I had to hold my old beliefs more loosely, less dogmatically. And sometimes, I had to let go of some beliefs completely. The tapestry of my Southern Baptist beliefs was beginning to unravel, a thread at a time.

I really enjoyed my first semester in college. This was a new beginning. I was leaving behind the social struggles of high school. In many ways,

I had a sense of being born anew. Nobody at college knew who I was, or, as I imagined, how others saw me. I made new friends, and I could stay up until I actually wanted to go to bed. I played a lot of ping-pong and pickup basketball games. Since I was away from home, and not constantly eating after dinner, I lost 20 pounds in the first three months. Plus, I was in a P.E. class that really challenged me. I actually won an award for the Most Physically improved that semester. The Alonzo Stagg Award for physical fitness. Because of the weight I lost, my mother thought I was ill.

I was in a dorm room with three other freshmen boys. I remember only one of their names, Wendell. With hindsight, I feel bad that Wendell got me for a roommate. He was a serious student. I would come in the room late at night, not so quietly, after playing around, which would wake him up. On more than one occasion, he confronted me about being more considerate of his need for sleep.

It was actually Wendell's good fortune that two significant events happened the next quarter that changed my life. First, my grades were so bad that I earned a spot on academic probation, which proved I really needed to take my grades more seriously. Second, and more importantly, I meet Joyce halfway through the next Winter quarter. She convinced me to learn to study. If I wanted to see her, I needed to meet her in the library, and I needed not to be playing around late into the night. I couldn't believe that Joyce, as cute as she was, actually liked me; I was smitten. In many ways, 61 years later, I still am.

Because I never learned how to study in high school, becoming a studious student didn't happen just because I wanted it to. My initial approach to improving my grades didn't include actually studying more. I had put a two-pronged plan into action before I met Joyce. I "reasoned" that I needed to take easier courses, which would assure me of A's and B's. The second part of my plan was that if it looked like I wasn't doing well in a course, I'd drop it before the last day to drop it. That way, dropping it would not hurt my GPA.

One of my easy courses was *Use of the Library*. On the first day of class, I quickly glanced over the syllabus and saw what needed to be completed and handed in, like understanding the Dewey Decimal System. This was going to be a piece of cake. So, I didn't really need to go to class

Doug and Joyce, Cascade College 1965

very often. However, what I had failed to notice was that the instructor, Miss Tish, graded on attendance. This hit me when I went to class toward the end of the semester, and Miss Tish addressed me when I waltzed into class. "Hello Mr. Henning, are you visiting us today?" OOPS! This was after the last day to drop a class. I got a 'D'. Result? My grades were actually more abysmal in the second quarter. At any rate, for Wendell's benefit, I was not coming in at all hours and waking him up.

I credit Joyce having encouraged me to learn how to study. She always wanted to meet in the library in the evenings. The first time she suggested meeting in the library, I wasn't at all sure where it was. I worried a bit about whether I'd be able to find her. Bear in mind, this was a small college with 90% of the classrooms, the administration offices, the chapel, and the library all in the same building. To put it mildly, I was a true non-academic geek. Joyce was, and still is, a true student. Since I didn't realize where the college library was, I walked to the Public Library, a couple of blocks from my dorm. I walked through the library, looking in all the nooks and crannies, but didn't see her. Men in love often have to resort to drastic measures. So I walked back to the campus and decided to go to the top story of the main building. I needed to see if maybe there was a library up there. Bingo! There was the library. I walked in and there she was, studying away.

I had a work-study job on campus to help pay for my tuition. I cleaned the bathrooms and showers in the gym, straightened up the small weight room and dust-mopped the basketball floor. A true serendipity of this job was that I got to know the basketball coach whose office was in the gym, Ray Burwick. Coach Burwick was a very likable man and became a role model of for me. He had a stutter that was worse than mine. But it didn't seem to bother him. Even when he would speak in the chapel, he would stutter his way through his speech as if his stutter wasn't even there. This really impressed me. I figured if he could speak without his stutter bothering him and not diminishing his effectiveness as a P.E. teacher, coach, or chapel speaker, then maybe I was making a bigger deal of it than necessary. I became the basketball team manager and traveled with the team, kept game statistics, and learned to tape ankles before practice and games. A freshman on the team was from Tacoma, and his parents were old friends of my parents. So, we often traveled together on the weekends to see our folks and do our laundry.

Joyce and I got married one year after we met: March 1966. Joyce was twenty-one, and I was twenty. Admittedly, with hindsight, this was much too young. But in March 2026, we will celebrate sixty years married. When asked what the secret of our success has been, we say we were lucky and that lust turned into a mature love. Plus, things in the mid-1960s were quite different. The Vietnam War was heating up, and all college men were feeling pressure from their local draft boards. Several of our friends got married just as young as we did, some have endured like ours, as far as we know, and others have not. We all thought that getting married was God's *will* for us. After all, we had prayed about it.

It's been said that Conservative Christianity's approach to reducing premarital sex and premarital pregnancy was to hand kids a wedding ring.

The average age at first marriage dipped into the early twenties during the 1950s. This is actually one contributor to the increase in divorce rates of the 1960s and 70s. People were getting married younger than their maturity level could handle. Interestingly, Conservative Christianity's answer to the surge in the divorce rate was to emphasize that divorce was a sin. A huge sin. Further, many, if not most, conservative Christian churches refused to marry people who had been previously married. Unlike other Christian groups, Conservative Christian denominations don't have an official hierarchy of sins. But if they did, divorce would be right at the top of the list. Although this has softened and changed in recent decades, many conservative Christian ministers still refuse to marry someone who has been divorced. This stance treated this issue like the unpardonable sin, rather than a mistake in judgment in being able to see how things might be far into the future.

A further irony of the 50% plus-or-minus divorce rate is that mate selection in the U.S. is a relatively random process. We can only be attracted to people we are in the same sphere we are in at the time we think we are ready to select a mate, like people in a class we are taking at college or in the same church we are in, who frequent the same bar we do. This is called the propinquity effect. So this rules out a vast number of people who might actually be a good match for us, but with whom we never come in contact. (It will be interesting to see whether the divorce rates decrease with the effect of online dating websites, which I assume will broaden the field from which to meet and select dating partners.) Add to this randomness of mate selection our infatuation with expecting to stay in a romantic state of love and not have to work out daily conflicts, like dealing with in-laws, who does what chores in the family, and so on. Divorce is not and never has been the unpardonable sin. I don't know of any other mistake or misjudgment that a person can make and be expected to pay for the rest of their lives.

So Joyce and I settled into newlywed married life. Joyce did her student-teaching, and by the end of that semester, she had signed a teaching contract for a fifth-grade job. I got a summer job working for Oregon State Grain Inspection. Ships and train boxcars unloaded loads of grain into silos, which were located along the river. My job was to climb up inside railroad boxcars loaded with grain, stick a probe deep into the grain to collect a sample, and then climb back down. Within a couple of weeks, I was having such difficulty breathing that I couldn't recline in bed at night. I went to the doctor, and after he examined me, he asked what I did for a job. I told him, and he told me to resign immediately. I had severe bronchial asthma. I had asthma as a kid, but I thought I had outgrown it.

After my breathing settled down, I was in the backyard of our house one day, hanging up our laundry. Our neighbor, Mr. Dobbs, Dobby, struck up a conversation and asked me if I needed a job. He was the foreman/supervisor of a tile setting company. They needed a tile setter's helper. Basically, a grunt. So I jumped at the chance. The next morning, I rode with him in his pickup truck to the job site in downtown Portland. He explained that the previous helper had gotten arrested and was in jail. The job was at a college dorm for Portland State University.

Dobby carefully explained the job to me: pour a bag of cement into the cement mixer, shovel in several loads of sand, add some water, and turn on the mixer. Simple enough, right? He placed a wheelbarrow in front of the mixer, and I dumped the load into the wheelbarrow. Then he pointed to a ramp of boards that went twenty feet up an incline and took a ninety-degree turn to the left up into the door of the building. He said the tile-setters would be waiting. He handed me a hard hat. So, I lifted the wheelbarrow's handles, got it balanced, and proceeded up the ramp. When I went to make the turn to the left, the heavy wheelbarrow's weight shifted. I lost my grip on the handles, stumbled to my knees, and the load of cement fell one story to a landing below. My hard hat fell off and followed the cement.

I got up, looked back at Dobby, and he motioned me to bring the wheelbarrow back down the ramp. I loaded another combination of cement and sand and dumped the load into the wheelbarrow. Then he had me pick up the wheelbarrow high enough so that the weight was on the wheel, not in my hands. He had me walk around behind the wheelbarrow as it almost propelled itself. About that time, a very big-looking construction guy walked up to me and handed me my hard hat. I delivered the concrete up the ramp and into the building. The tile setters greeted me with a smile and showed me where to dump it. I returned down the ramp to get another load.

I asked Dobby why he hadn't shown me how to operate the wheelbarrow the first time. He taught me one of several lessons I've never forgotten. He said, "I don't like saying things twice. If I had shown you the first time, you wouldn't have paid careful attention, you would have dropped it just like you did. Then I'd have to tell it to you all over again."

He really had my attention. This was one of those threads that would run throughout my life.

Mr and Mrs Dobbs became like parents to us and frequently had us over for dinner in the evening. I got proficient at operating a loaded wheelbarrow. I got fast enough at the job so that when the other helper got arrested and landed in jail, I supplied two tile setters in two different locations at an elementary school later in the summer. I was running with the loaded wheelbarrow.

During the summer, Joyce got a job at a local breakfast-and-lunch diner a few blocks from our house. So, on Saturdays, when I wasn't working, I'd go to the diner and sit at the counter, and the owner would allow me to eat for free. On occasion, I'd also wash dishes, pots, and pans. One Saturday, I was sitting there, and a big, construction-looking guy sat down beside me. He said, aren't you that little hod carrier that runs with loaded wheelbarrows at that elementary school south of Portland? Yep! That's me. By the end of the summer, I was lean but still not very mean.

chapter 4

New Threads <u>for</u> the Tapestry

Greetings from Your Military Draft Board. You've been selected.
During the mid-sixties, when we got married, the Vietnam War was really heating up. The talk around the student union on many mornings was about who had recently received their draft notice or decided to enlist. (Because our college was so small, losing even a few students was a big deal and hurt the college financially.) So by 1968, the college had to close its doors, and records merged with a couple of other Christian colleges in the Northwest.) Despite my belief that it was not God's will that I would be drafted, eleven months after our wedding, in mid-February 1967, my draft notice was in the mailbox. I remember standing at our front door and staring at the letter. No matter how long I stared, it continued to say the same thing—*greetings from the United States Government. You have been selected to serve in the U.S. Army.*

Although I appealed to my draft board that I was a full-time student in the middle of my Junior year and married, they didn't find my arguments compelling. Even though my study habits had improved and my grade point average was gradually rising, the draft board concluded that I was not a serious enough student to warrant a student deferment. Each draft board, prior to the lottery system, had a quota they had to fill. So, by 1967, they were looking for warm bodies that could walk straight and pass a minimal physical exam. Even though I had been diagnosed with asthma and had to actually quit the job I had at a grain inspection center in Portland due to my asthma, the draft really wanted me. In many ways, this felt like an ultimate failure on several levels. I wasn't even smart enough to hold on to my college deferment.

I believed you were either smart or not. It had not occurred to me that a crucial element of intelligence was knowing how to learn. It actually took me a while to get this from my head down to my heart, so that I really believed this about myself.

I should say I'm convinced, based on my immaturity described above, that had it not been for getting drafted and going into the Air Force, Joyce and I may not have been able to stay married.

I heard years ago that one of the major hurdles for young married couples is getting through the first few years with an immature male. The military helped me grow up fast and get serious about life. I hope that some of those reading this understand that it is never really too late to turn things around. Granted, we can't turn back the calendar, and there will always be the reaping of what has been sown, but new beginnings are always possible.

Further, at times, the situations that come our way appear to be horrible, and we even feel like our life as we know it has come to an end. Yet, depending on how we choose to respond to the apparent tragedy, a newness of life can and will emerge. This is one of the things I really liked about working in rehabilitation settings and doing psychology. I got the rare opportunity to be a part of someone's life when they thought they were at the bottom. And then help and watch them climb out of the pit to new life. C. S. Lewis, in his book "Miracles", asserts that this is the pattern of real miracles. Greater than physical healing is this decent and re-ascent—going down to come up—which is part of our human nature.[1] The ability to recover from being really down.

The only concession the draft board offered was to allow me to finish the academic quarter, which ended in mid-March. They essentially canceled the draft notice and promised to send me another one in the third week of March. It was common knowledge that new draftees, following

---

[1]. Lewis, C.S. (1947) *Miracles,* Harper San Francisco

an abbreviated, six-week rather than eight-week Basic Training, quickly found themselves pounding the ground in Vietnam. Due to a lack of experience and insufficient training, their life expectancy on the battlefield wasn't very long. So I scrambled and found an Air Force Recruiter, a friend of my father who attended his church. He had me take an aptitude test. If I could score high enough—above 90%—on the math portion, he would be able to get me enlisted before my second draft notice arrived. I must admit that I was not too hopeful of getting the required score. One of the courses that had prevented my GPA from rising quickly was Statistics. I had just flunked Statistics the quarter before. But miracle of miracles, I got a ninety-five percent, and I was in. My enlistment in the Air Force was a delayed enlistment. This gave me essentially three months before going to basic training. I finished the Winter Quarter and did not re-enroll for Spring. I stopped in to see my Statistics professor to show him my draft notice and enlistment in the Air Force. I was actually hoping he would feel a little guilty for giving me an F. Instead, he responded that he thought going into the military would do me some good. He couldn't have been more right.

In addition to cleaning the gym, I also had a job driving a laundry truck to pick up dirty laundry and deliver clean laundry to three laundry stores around Portland. This job paid $75.00 a month, which covered our rent. I also went to work full-time for the tile-setting company so we could pay down our bills as much as possible before going off to Texas for Basic Training—we had a car loan and a school loan. Joyce was in her first year of teaching. Together we were able to get ahead financially to make it through the first several months of the low Airmen's pay while I was in Tech School—$90.00 a month.

If going off to college at 19 was a form of social new birth for me, being drafted into the military was a new birth for my intellect, character, and maturity. I had absolutely no idea of what to expect at Basic. Because I was still struggling a bit with asthma I assumed, and rightfully so, that it would be demanding physically. So as soon as I enlisted, I began running a couple of miles a day after working, with ankle weights on. I had read in a pamphlet about Lackland Air Force Base, where I would be doing Basic Training. I saw that they had a nice golf course, So, I asked the recruiter if I should take my clubs with me? I actually kept a straight face and said he thought they would have clubs I could use. It only took me a couple of days to realize I probably wouldn't have any spare time to recreate. We arrived on Saturday afternoon. The Training Instructor (TI) told us we were going to have a G.I. party. I thought, How nice, a welcoming party. So we got out the buckets and mops and scrubbed everything. Actually, everything looked quite clean with no need for cleaning, but we scrubbed anyway, then did it again. Then the next morning, at four a.m., the TI walked through the open bay barracks, banging a tin garbage can lid with a hammer and yelling, *"Fall Out."* Our day had begun.

TECH SCHOOL - Biloxi, Mississippi (1967)

Following Basic Training, I was assigned to Keesler AFB, Biloxi, Mississippi, for a year of Tech School. Because Joyce was able to get a teaching job in Mississippi, she could join me in Biloxi. The State of Mississippi did not require a teaching degree, or any college degree for that matter, to get a teaching job. Because she had an elementary teaching degree, they hired her based on a letter and transcript from the Oregon College of Education. They called her and hired her over the phone.

Living in the Deep South in 1968 was our first exposure as adults to overt racism. Drinking fountains were labeled Colored or White. Restaurants had signs prohibiting Negros. Black Airmen had their own seg-regated barracks. The fifth-grade class that Joyce taught was in Gulfport, just down the road from Biloxi. This was where most Air Force officers lived with their families. Early in the school year, a black family moved into the district. The principal explained to Joyce that "since she was from the north, the only black student would be in her class". His name was Robert. As was the case throughout Joyce's 40-plus-year teaching career, we attended her students' after-school activities, including Robert's baseball games. League baseball was segregated. We were in the deep south, and we were the only white people at his games. We attended all of his baseball games. Without realizing the "why," sitting in the small bleachers was as if we had an insu-lating bubble around us; no one sat close to us. All the same, Robert seemed to appreciate his teacher's interest in him and attendance at his games. With hindsight, we should have asked if it was okay with his parents to be there. We just naively assumed that being the only white people there, at a gathering of black people, was OK. What naive arrogance.

Electronics Tech school, and later Electronic Counter Measures (ECM), I realized that I might be smarter than I had displayed in High School and my first try at college. The motivation to do well was clear. Rumors were that if we failed to pass exams at the end of each section, we would be transferred to other, and likely more dangerous, career fields that would put us on the fast track to get us sent rapidly to Vietnam. I performed at the top of my class in each course.

My day began early. We had to be in formation by 5:00 a.m., in front of the Squadron headquarters for morning inspection. Joyce and I lived a few blocks from the side gate of Keesler Air Force Base. It was about a half-hour walk from the house to the Squadron on the other side of the airfield flight-line. In winter in Biloxi on the Gulf Coast, it was always damp, which translated into chilly temperatures with wind chills below freezing. At least one day a week we had a break-starch inspection. This meant we had to break starch and put on newly laundered fatigues that were starched so heavily that the sleeves and pant legs were stuck together. (On the other inspection days, we only had to iron the fatigues that we had worn the day before.) For those of us who lived off base with our wives, this meant we had to walk stiffly until we got to the squadron so the creases in the fatigues looked as good as the guys who lived in the squadron barracks. If we looked wrinkled, we were in danger of getting "gigs"—demerits. Once your name was on the gig list, it never came off. The gig list was used to assign extra duty on evenings and weekends around the base. In addition to breaking starch, our boots had to be spit-shined so that you could see your reflection.

All of this to say, Joyce couldn't drive me to the base because, sitting in the car would have meant the creases in the fatigues would bend. Plus, on inspection day, we couldn't wear our fatigue jackets because they would wrinkle the creases. So I would walk stiffly, a half-hour in the chilly, damp weather, to the squadron. But I looked like a sharp troop!

When I finished tech school in June 1968, I had to out-process at various offices around the base and have a form signed that I wasn't taking anything, I shouldn't or owed any fines. One of those offices was the squadron office. I walked in and handed the sergeant my form for him to sign. He looked through various files, then looked again, and finally said I don't have your name on any lists, like the gig list. That's not possible? It doesn't even look like you were here. I smiled and said, "I know, no gigs for the last ten months, Sarge."

As I said, I was a sharp troop! I never pulled extra duty.

Following tech school in June 1968, we went to Mountain Home AFB in Idaho. On our drive to Mountain Home, we heard on the car radio that Robert F. Kennedy had just been assassinated while making a presidential campaign speech in Los Angeles. Martin Luther King Jr. had been assassinated just two months before. What was going on? This was 1968. The Chicago riots at the National Democratic Convention would erupt two months later. Police brutality would be extreme. Most of the protests were over the war in Vietnam. There was also much racial unrest during that time. George Wallace, Alabama Governor and staunch segregationist, threatened to run over any protesters who tried to stop him by lying down in front of his car. Unbeknownst to me, in a little over four months, I was heading to that war. This was a crazy and chaotic time for the U.S. and for us personally. We were in the middle of so much ourselves that we were unable to grasp the impact of everything happening around us.

It's been said that if one remembers 1968 with much detail and clarity, then they weren't there. This marked the culmination of much unrest in the society of the United States. Some historians refer to this period, which began in the early 1960s and ended in 1972, as the long 68, which was actually ongoing throughout Western Europe as well.[2]

Oblivious to the impact all of this was about to have on us, we were excited to be going to the Pacific Northwest. It was only a day's drive to our parents in Eugene, Oregon, and Tacoma, Washington. We arrived on June 25, found a small house to rent, and were looking forward to a pleasant stay in the North West. It was a common, if unwarranted, assumption that the Air Force left its airmen in one place for about a year

---

2. Vinen, Richard (2018) *The Long 68: Radical Protest and Its Enemies*, Penguin Random House, UK

before moving them again—in the same year. Joyce got a teaching job, and I got a fishing license. We were all set.

The first week in July, I got orders for the Vietnam War, stationed in Thailand, leaving on October 26 from San Francisco—I was leaving a day before my birthday. It was explained that the new "fiscal" year started in July, so technically, it was "next year." I couldn't believe it. Like my belief that it would not be God's will that I would get drafted, I had been sure I wouldn't have to go to war. I was learning that just because people cloaked their selfish desires in things like "it's God's will," didn't make it so.

Joyce was able to quickly get out of her teaching contract. At the end of September, we took a one-month leave, moved to Tacoma, and stayed with my parents. Joyce got on substitute teacher lists for several of the school districts around Tacoma. On October 26, I flew to Travis AFB in San Francisco and flew out to Bangkok.

Because we crossed the international date line on the way to Thailand, I left on the 26th and landed on the 28th. I completely and literally missed the 27th, my birthday. A common saying in the military when thinking about the worst that could happen for a particular incident was, "What are they going to do, take away your birthday"? Well, that's what happened. They took away my 23rd birthday. We changed planes in Bangkok and flew north to Udorn Royal Thai AFB. When I stepped off the plane, the first thing I saw was rice paddies that went forever. My first thought was, I don't know if I can do this.

I was in-processed and assigned to my barracks. These were open-bay barracks: no interior walls, upright lockers divided one bunk-bed area from the next. Because of the tropical climate, the exterior walls were screen material. My bunkmate was Nate Carey. He introduced himself and, right off the bat, asked if I was a Christian. If I were, he would take me downtown and introduce me to a white-haired missionary lady, Nina Miller, who ran a serviceman's center—a gathering place for G.I.'s. Over the next months, I would meet several other G.I.s who were in the same situation I was in: G.I.s who were not interested in drinking heavily and running with the town prostitutes. Nina was a grandmotherly, sweet lady from Topeka, Kansas. Her husband had died, and she subsequently felt called to Udon Thani, Thailand, to minister to G.I.s at the AFB.

I credit the servicemen's center for keeping me sane during the year I was there. During the New Year's Eve gathering at the Hospitality home, I became a Christian as an adult. The denominational leanings of the men, and of Nina, were Charismatic/Assembly of God. This was quite a change from my Southern Baptist upbringing and my college exposure to Wesleyanism. I was adding Pentecostalism to my faith. I'm sure some of my dead Baptist relatives were, not for the first time, turning over in their graves.

Nate, my bunkmate, was getting ready to leave for stateside in a couple of weeks and gave me his bicycle. Nate told me he was a distant nephew of William Carrey, an anthropologist and missionary to India in the late 1790s. Just as Nate was leaving, I was notified that I had been assigned to the wrong barracks, and so I moved to the one where several of the guys who worked in my shop lived. Given the role that Nina Miller and the servicemen's center played in my life, .I've thought that meeting Nate by the "mistake" of being in the wrong barracks was not just a coincidence but somehow an act of providence.

One month into my tour, I got a letter from Joyce saying she was pregnant. I was so very excited and at the same time disappointed, to say the least. I was going to miss the pregnancy and delivery of our first child, and Joyce was going through it alone. By this time, I was getting used to not being surprised by things that were coming up in my life—getting drafted, going to war, missing the pregnancy and delivery of my son Scott.

Even though I was good at my job, I soon became disillusioned with what the U.S. was doing in Southeast Asia on more than one level. We had butted our noses into a civil war, killing hundreds of thousands of Vietnamese. Fifty-eight thousand American G.I.s, and counting, died because of combat, many more would die in the coming decades from exposure to toxic defoliants like Agent Orange and from suicide.[3] In the end, North and South Vietnam would be united anyway. Locally, around

---

3. "22 a day" has become a rallying cry for groups calling for better mental health care for veterans. Although the number varies depending on the year the data is gathered, the rate it has consistently run between 18-22 veterans commit suicide every day for the last 20 years. Suicide rates for non-veteran groups is around 12%-13%. During this same time the prevalence of mental health or substance use disorders rose from 28% 42% for those veterans using Veterans Health Administration.

Working on ECM

Climbing into the tail

Udon Thani, the Communists were teaching local farmers how to farm. They were winning the hearts and minds of the people. Besides bombing the bejesus out of an impoverished country, our G.I.s were helping spread sexually transmitted diseases and getting young girls pregnant before returning to the States—leaving the girls and their babies to fend for themselves.

I worked the night shift, 10:30 p.m. to 8:30 a.m., for the year I was in Thailand. I really preferred this shift because the higher-ranking officers and NCOs weren't around much. So, all we had to do was repair and modify the Electronic Countermeasures (ECM) equipment on the F-4E Phantom II fighter-bomber aircraft. ECM equipment was relatively new in the mid to late 60s. The purpose of this equipment was to warn the pilot that they were being tracked by enemy radar, and just as importantly, what direction the bullets, rockets, and missiles were coming from, so they could take evasive action.

The downside of the night shift was that it was very hot and humid during the day, so it was always difficult to sleep during the day. We were always sleep-deprived. Sometimes, when I was particularly tired, during a lunch break, at night, I'd go out the front of the shop and get on a shuttle bus that circled the base perimeter. It took about half an hour to make the loop. I'd lie down on the bench in the back and quickly fall asleep. The bus would make its way back to my shop in half an hour, and the driver would wake me up. This is when I also learned to drink coffee. The thirty-cup coffee urn had made its first pot in the morning when the bosses arrived at eight a.m. Then, each time it ran dry, they wouldn't empty the grounds. In the name of conservation, we'd just throw in another one cup of grounds on top of the old grounds and fill it up with water. So, by around four in the morning, the coffee was thick as mud, with about the same taste. I'm sure if we had let a spoon stand in a cup very long, it would have eventually disintegrated. When I finally had a taste of regular coffee, I was surprised by how pleasant it actually tasted.

We spent a lot of time on the flight line, troubleshooting problems on the planes and getting them ready for their next sortie (mission). The equipment was all solid-state and, as such, not prone to breaking inside the black boxes in which it was housed. The most common problems occurred at electrical connectors and junctions that connected one part of the plane, via a bulkhead, to the next section. These wires passed through the bulkhead connections and often came loose or broke due to jet engine vibrations. But due to the tight spaces where the equipment and wiring were located, getting to them was a challenge. Bundles of cables would pass through one cannon plug connector to the other side of a bulkhead. To repair these connectors, we had to unplug them, which required strong hands. So doing fingertip pushups to strengthen my hands was a daily exercise throughout my time in the Air Force and often a regular part of my workout after that.

However, about 15 years ago, when I started riding my bike a couple of hours at a time, I began noticing numbness in my hands at the end of a ride. So I saw a hand surgeon. Turns out the Scaphoid Carpals of both hands, at the base of the thumb, were chipped, cracked, and worn down. He said it was odd that both hands would have symmetrical wear and injury like that. It looked like thirty or forty years ago, I had either been in an accident where I landed hard on both hands or somehow injured them. It wasn't until just recently that I made the connection between the wear and tear I experience now and doing finger-tip pushups for several years, and the need for reconstructive surgery on both hands several years ago. In the surgery they he removed a carpel and rebuilt the thumbs as best he could. Now my hands are anything but strong. Joyce has to open water bottles and jars.

So there were always planes running their engines close to ours. Frequently, the plane I was working on was running its engines and waiting to get the ECM equipment fixed. This and the B-52s I worked on when I returned to the States is why I'm totally deaf today. My hearing declined gradually from the time I was 23. Because my deafness is acquired and has progressed gradually, as opposed to genetic, I didn't really notice it until I was in my mid-40s. So in the early 90s, when the audiologist asked me if I had ever been around loud noises, I just chuckled and said yes.

I was good at what I did and received the Air Force Commendation Medal for my work in Thailand. Frequently, when working on a piece of equipment in the shop, a couple of new pilots, young second and first lieutenants, were taking a tour of the various equipment shops to learn about the most recent modifications of the equipment on the planes they would be flying. All ECM equipment was in Southeast Asia; none was in the United States. So, the new pilots would not have been familiar with ECM. Often, the younger pilots had a cocky attitude and acted as if they knew it all. So, when someone like me, a lowly two-striper, began instructing them, they didn't pay much attention. Then, after a couple of missions over enemy territory with anti-aircraft guns firing at them and an occasional surface-to-air missile (SAM) flying by them, they would come back to the shop, and with a sense of humility, ask if we could explain the equipment to them again. (Probably similar to me learning how to run a wheelbarrow.) It's pretty scary to have anti-aircraft (A.A.) shells being shot at them and know that SAMs, the size of telephone poles, are tracking them. A Major, who was an experienced F-4 pilot and friend, often hung out at the Hospitality Home in downtown Udonthani. He talked about how scary it was to have near misses by SAMs with AA tracers lighting up the night sky.

The Air Force keeps meticulous records, ad nauseam, not just in duplicate but in multiple places. We had a whiteboard listing the tail numbers of each phantom whose equipment we had an outstanding work order, as well as its upcoming sortie schedule. The Sergeant kept a three-by-five card file on his desk for each plane we were working on, sometimes awaiting parts; the captain kept a similar, separate card file on his desk. There was also a loose-leaf notebook for the shift supervisor. Redundancy was the name of the game. When we completed working on a piece of equipment, we were supposed to make a note on each board, card file, and notebook. We also had to make notes in the parts room when we removed a part so that new parts could be ordered. (Some parts were hard to get from the states, especially if we didn't order them very often. Due to the part's high price, we weren't allowed to keep too many backups on hand. One part was a multiport coaxial cable connector. So every now and then, to show usage, one of us would go into the parts bin and take a couple of connectors out and smash them with a hammer.) Once the work was completed, and the unit had been reinstalled on the aircraft, we made notes on the Crew Chief's log where the plane was docked. This was "completing the work order".

With all these duplications of cards, logs, and the large whiteboard, it was not uncommon for whoever had done the work to forget, or assume someone else had made the rounds to each place where the records were kept, like the sergeant's and the captain's card files. Most of us figured they could look at the whiteboards and get updated the way we did. This was especially the case when the turnaround time for an aircraft was short and we had several jobs going at the same time. The main records that we always remembered to document were the whiteboard and the Crew Chief's log.

So when we got bored on the night shift and wanted to cause a little havoc, one of us, most often a short-timer, would look at the whiteboard, and see which aircraft was due to fly in an hour or so. And go to the shift supervisor or the captain's log and pull that plane's card, which usually hadn't been updated, and say loud enough that all could hear, "hey Sarge, it looks like number so and so is due to fly, but the work isn't complete." The Sarge and a few others would go bat-shit for several minutes until they saw that the other records had been filled out. Then they would rant about how this was "just like taking a crap, the job isn't done until the paperwork is finished." Admittedly, this wasn't always kind to the guys in charge, but it did provide some cheap entertainment.

Before Nate Carey, my wrong bunkmate in the wrong barracks, left to return stateside, he gave me his bike and introduced me to a Thai teacher at a local trade school in Udon Thani. One class she taught was English. If I were so inclined, I could take his place, helping her teach conversational English. Since I was working the night shift on the base, and the days were much too hot to get any sleep, I rode my bike to town a couple of days a week to help her teach. I really enjoyed doing this.

A couple of weeks before I was to return home, the teacher's husband, who was a colonel in the Royal Thai Air Force, picked me up on the back of his motorcycle. I had just gotten off duty. As a thank-you for helping her teach, they invited me to their bungalow for brunch and to meet their young children. I wish I had stayed in touch with her and her family. But when I left to come home, the only thing I could think of was getting home, settling back into being a husband, and getting to know my three-month-old son, Scott.

I, along with some of the other G.I.s, who frequented the Christian Hospitality Home, often visited an orphanage for Thai-American babies and toddlers. Since they were mixed-race, Thai people often shunned them. G.I.'s girlfriends would be pregnant or already have a child when the G.I. returned stateside. There was one cute and adorable little boy named John, whom I often held and played with. I would have tried to adopt John had Joyce not just given birth to Scott. I've sometimes wondered how those babies' lives have turned out. They would be in their 50s now.

So, even though it was largely subconscious, I found myself immersed in Thai culture as much as possible. I felt the need to do some good instead of the war we were waging on all of Southeast Asia, targeting a significant portion of it. *There was actually an "Operation Baby Lift" at the end of the war to get as many babies out of Vietnam as possible. There is a very tender picture of babies lying on seats and strapped in on a chartered Pan Am 747 used to transport as many babies as possible from Saigon to the U.S.* [4]

---

4. Clarke, Thurston (2019) *Honorable Exit: How a Few Brave Americans Risked All to Save our Vietnamese Allies at the End of the War.* Double Day Random House, U.S.A.

Udon Thani

I realize this may not be a popular view of our role in Southeast Asia, but the older I've gotten and the more I've read and studied East Asia, *the more I have struggled with a sense of moral injury. That is, my role in the Air Force was against my personal moral code. As young airmen and soldiers, we were used to blow up a part of the world that is among the world's poorest people. I believe that what we were doing was morally wrong. My occasional PTSD symptoms, which surfaced in the mid-1980s, have made my life unpleasant at times as it has for many, many other veterans. So, even though I was not a combat soldier, it's the knowledge that I participated in something very immoral that weighs on me. This has taken an intellectual and emotional toll. Buddhism has helped me forgive that earlier version of myself and realize that I'm not that person any longer.*

The people of Southeast Asia seemed to me to be kind in their Buddhist beliefs and ways. I'll speak more specifically about Buddhism's impact on me later. Although I would not say that I have become a total pacifist, I definitely am anti-war. I heard psychiatrist and author M. Scott Peck speak at a Christian Psychology conference in the 1980s. Dr. Peck had recently become a Christian and said he realized that as a Christian, he needed to stop smoking. He also said he realized that conservative Christians were often pro-war, which he was not. He conceded that as long as we live in the world, we sometimes have no choice. Personally, I think that the U.S. jumps into war and other international violence almost reflexively. Granted, we, the public, are not aware of much of what goes on before troops are sent in, or we begin bombing another part of the world. And, as I understand it, there are efforts on behalf of the U.S. to keep peace in certain regions of the world. Yet, these peacekeeping missions get relatively little press. Early in his Army career as a physician, my son, Scott, was stationed at a U.N. Base in Kosovo as part of a peacekeeping effort. Part of his work was to travel into the country, often with local doctors, to treat people in local villages.

Despite the few non-war efforts, the U.S. tends to lean heavily into warmongering.

While in Thailand, I was also involved in was an organization associated with the on-base chapel. I was elected president of the Protest Men of the Chapel (PMOC). The reason I was elected president was that I was not in the room to object when the men were choosing someone. As president, this meant I helped organize meetings and decide how to use the money collected at our meetings. A few of us had gotten to know a missionary doctor who had a clinic about an hour south of Udorn. We would travel by train, which was an experience in and of itself. On those trips, we would take him the offering money that we had collected. One of the many diseases he treated was leprosy. His house, made of wood and bamboo, was on stilts and was attached to the clinic. I can still see it in my mind's eye. It reminded me of a small veterinary office: a stainless steel table and cabinets. Certainly no frills. But he was doing what he could do with what he had. He was supported by the Christian Missionary Alliance (CMA) church. There were several CMA missionaries in that region of Thailand.

COMING HOME A NEW Thread

The stated intention of the Air Force at that time was that, given our role in the war, Southeast Asia returnees would get their base of choice when they returned to the States. Just in case we didn't get our first choice, we should also put down a couple of others as backups. So, being from Tacoma, I put in for McCord AFB in Tacoma, Mountain Home AFB in Idaho, and Fairchild AFB in Spokane, Washington. When news came that orders had come down and were in the squadron office, we all raced to open our mailboxes in the Charge of Quarters (CQ) office. I remember it as clearly as if it happened just a few days ago. I had to sit down. I stared at it much the way I had stared at my draft notice thirty months before. I had gotten Minot, North Dakota. I often joked that the Air Force almost missed my country of choice. Forty more miles, and I would have been in Canada.

A bit of Air Force folklore was that Minot was one of those bases people got sent to when they had made someone mad or committed a grave mistake. But I quickly regained my composure and reminded myself that I was going home. If Joyce and Scott were there with me, any place would be great. So, on October 27, my birthday, I walked out the back of our ECM shop and boarded a plane for Bangkok, transferred to a chartered plane, and headed for San Francisco. Sixteen hours later, we circled the San Francisco airport; the pilot played Tony Bennett's 'I Left My Heart in San Francisco'; we all got tears in our eyes, and we landed. I left Udorn on October 27, 1969, and landed the next day. I got back my missed birthday from the year before. Being home was like having a double birthday—truly the best birthday present ever.

Joyce flew to San Francisco to meet me. When the G.I.s were returning home from the war, we were told to wear our dress uniforms when we left Udorn. However, because of the strong anti-war sentiment and demonstrations in the states, we were told not to be seen in public in our uniforms, especially in liberal San Francisco. So I quickly ducked into the closest men's room and changed into my civvies—civilian clothes as opposed to military uniforms. Then, I made my way to meet the plane from Portland. There she was, just as pretty as I had left her.

We stayed a few days in San Francisco among the long-haired hippies. Because of my disillusionment with the war, I was happy to be among people I believed saw things the way I did. But worried that my very short hair might suggest I was not one of them. When we flew back to Portland, my parents and Joyce's parents, holding Scott, were at the gate. I remember the outfit Scott was wearing as clear as day. It was, a little red and black checked suit and he looked wonderful. Joyce had left instructions with her parents to hand Scott to me as soon as I got off the plane, which they did. I was home!!

WHY NOT MINOT

A couple of weeks after getting home, we drove to Minot ("Why not Minot?" was the often-spoken cry), and I spent the next twenty months working on B-52s. The day we pulled into Minot, it was twenty below zero with a horizontal snowstorm. It was said that it never really snowed in North Dakota. It just snowed in Montana and then blew to Minnesota. Having just come from Thailand, where it was so hot that you could get sunburned through a t-shirt, I wondered if I would ever warm up. When we got to Minot, housing was so tight that if you waited for the newspaper to hit the newsstands in the morning, the houses and apartments would already be rented. So we made it a habit to go to the newspaper office to get the latest edition—hot off the press. Some families were actually living in uninsulated garages.

We eventually found an apartment. It was a one-bedroom upper-floor apartment. Unbeknownst to us, the landlord, to save money, had a governor on the furnace so that the temperature never got above 60 degrees during the day and so low at night that ice formed on the inside of the windows. We had to have Scott sleep with us to keep him warm. A few months later, we found another place to live. We had met a couple at the Southern Baptist church in town—Dan and Pat. Dan had just gotten out of the Marines and was attending the local college in Minot. They had been keeping their eye out for a better living arrangement for us. They were moving into a basement apartment that had the middle-floor apartment of the house available. We grabbed it immediately. The middle floor would be warmer. Even so, Scott got pneumonia that first year. It was bitterly cold. Some single G.I.s had been renting the house before us. The house was full of garbage, shotgun holes in the front door from rowdy, inebriated G.I.s, and empty beer cans stacked to the ceiling with bags of trash everywhere—so we spent the first week cleaning out the mess, which included burning the trash in burn barrels outside.

The first weekend we were in our new apartment, late at night, a couple of guys were knocking on the door to let them in. They were ready to party. I told them to go away. They started driving circles around the house, honking their horns. I called the police. When they got there, the guys had left. The cop was in an unmarked Pontiac GTO. He said he would wait, that they would be back. He knew the house had a reputation for wild parties. He hid behind the house. Sure enough, the guys returned. He turned on his flashing lights and got out to talk to them. He told us they wouldn't be bothering us anymore. They didn't.

One evening, when I got home, before taking off my parka, I took out several bags of trash, placed them in the three barrels, and lit each one. I walked back by them on the way to the house and looked at each one to be sure the fire had lit the trash. Just as I looked in one barrel, an explosion occurred, and my hair and uniform were immediately on fire. I quickly threw myself into the snow and rolled to put the fire out. Joyce had heard the explosion and seen the fiery flash. She looked out the window, saw me on the ground, and thought the explosion had knocked me down. Thankfully, it was not as bad as it could have been.

The explosion had been from an aerosol can of red spray paint. My face was covered with hot, fiery red paint. Since we were nineteen miles from the base, we figured it was too far to drive to the base hospital. Joyce drove me to the local hospital emergency room. They were concerned that my burns were third-degree and the boiling vapors had gotten into my lungs. (Knowing I had asthma just added to the concern.) So, I spent the next several days in the hospital in isolation. Fortunately, if there is a silver lining, a recently developed Sulfamylon cream was available to treat napalm burns in Vietnam. Thankfully, my lungs were unharmed, and for the next few months, I washed my face and scalp daily with a special soap and applied the cream. Since the burns turned out to be only a little worse than second-degree burns, no skin grafts were required, and, contrary to initial concerns, I was not permanently tattooed with red paint on my face. I did smell of burnt hair and skin for a few months afterward. If you look closely enough, one eyebrow is shorter than the other.

One other unique Air Force experience for me: One late evening in the spring, I was installing a hundred-pound transmitter in a panel on the outside of the bomber. North Dakota had some spectacular lightning storms in the spring. I had a stand jacked up about fifteen feet next to the panel I had taken off. It was raining torrents and lightning like crazy. Because this piece of equipment was heavy, I was leaning on the stand's rail and using it to push the equipment into its slot when lightning struck the tail of the plane. Yes, the plane had grounding straps hooked all over it, but for whatever reason, my hand on the transmitter and my right elbow resting on the railing of the metal stand served as an additional grounding strap. A shot of lightning electricity went down my right forearm. It scared the shit out of me and hurt like hell. After I collected myself, I secured the transmitter into place, picked up my tool bag, climbed down the ladder, and went to the line truck, which was waiting to take me back to the shop. The crew chief was also waiting for me. He pointed out that I wasn't finished because the panel door was still open. I looked at him and asked him if he had seen the lightning strike. He laughed and said yes, it had scared him and the truck driver. I showed him my hand, which was still cramped. I was a short-timer by then and really didn't care what they did. I told him I was going back to the shop, that he could climb up and close the panel, and that the truck driver would be back for him after he dropped me off. They had already taken my birthday away from me once, and I was already in Minot, so I wasn't too concerned.

A couple of months into our first spring in Minot, our names had worked their way down the waiting list, and we could move on-base to a two-story four-plex. Joyce got a teaching job at the elementary school on base.

Most of the ECM equipment on the B-52s was similar enough to what had been on the Phantoms. So, I settled into working on the big planes. Only when temperatures and wind chill got below seventy-five degrees below zero were we allowed to stay in the shop, unless, of course, there was a Special Operations practice going on, which we had from time to time.

As an aside, when we lived in Kansas in the 1990s, I heard of a radio station in North Dakota that played a song by a local musician during an especially cold snap—"40 below keeps the riffraff out". Crime rates dropped during the frigid winters. It was often colder in Minot than in places in Alaska. The actual temperature could run twenty-five degrees below zero for a few weeks in a row. Then, when the temperature climbed to a little above zero, it felt like a heat wave. One of our neighbors on base was from Florida. He was so excited about the warm snap that he went out to wash his car, not realizing it was still around zero. He threw some soapy water on his car, and of course, it froze immediately. He had frozen soapy water on his car and a cracked windshield.

I was not the only one who had to work outside in sub-zero weather. Women teachers weren't allowed to wear slacks. This was the early seventies in conservative North Dakota, so they were required to wear dresses or skirts. Maybe not such a big deal if they weren't also required to take the kids out to recess when it was 25 below zero. It took so long to get the kids ' cold-weather gear on that they only had a short time to actually play. So, along with many pleasant and not-so-pleasant memories, Joyce got frostbite on her knees.

When the Red Cross notified me in Thailand that Scott had been born, I started worrying about whether I would be a good dad. I realized that how we learn to be adults is, in large part, due to the modeling our parents did for us. My dad was a nice man, charming and a good storyteller. As a result, he was well-liked by other adults, especially in our church. People would sometimes say to me that it must be great to have a dad like mine. But the truth was that I didn't feel like I had a "close" relationship with him or my mother. I'm not completely sure why that was the case, but I have a couple of theories. First, my dad was a churchman, but to a fault. Church always seemed to come first. Even through my teen years, I was envious of friends in the church who would occasionally miss Sunday Evening services to stay home because they had planned a family outing that extended into the late afternoon, or just to be together. Even when we would go on weekends or longer extended vacations, my dad would always find a local Southern Baptist church so we could attend and not miss going to church. In Tacoma, my dad and I were on a bowling team together, but it was in a church league. The team was our own church members. Church seemed to be everywhere. With hindsight, I believe our ultra-church commitments contributed to a lack of depth in our relationships.

My second theory as to why I was not close to my parents was that I was 7 or 8 years older than my two sisters. My mom had had a miscarriage when I was four years old. That instance of my dad quickly taking me to the neighbor's house in the middle of the night and rushing my mom to the hospital is fairly vivid in my memory. I remember standing with my dad on the sidewalk of the hospital where my mom was in and waving to her. So, with hindsight, the fact that they had been having trouble getting pregnant was pretty obvious. When my sisters finally came along, fourteen months apart, my parents were elated.

My sisters were both blond, and people assumed they were twins. Because I was seven and eight years older, mom and dad seemed to believe I could get along without a lot of attention. The "joke" my dad would often tell was that Dawn, my oldest sister, had my dad. Noel, my youngest sister, had my mom, and I had the dog, Pettie. That Dawn was my dad's favorite, and Noel was my mom's favorite, *was very apparent.*

So, in the middle of Vietnam, I began worrying whether I could be a good dad when I finally got home from Thailand. Being good Southern Baptists, we found a Southern Baptist church as soon as we moved to Minot. The church mostly military families, especially the young adult Sunday School group. I clearly remember, fifty-five years later, one potluck dinner when we met at a house on base. Scott was beginning to walk. He was also starting to talk and would walk around saying, 'Excuse me, excuse me,' which clearly added to the cute factor. As such, everyone seemed to look out for him. I was watching another dad who had a three kids. I was impressed by how good he seemed to be with his youngest son, who was a little older than Scott. I really liked how he attended to his boy: he was tender and kind. The dad's nickname was "Jeep." I decided to watch Jeep at every opportunity and strive to be like him. I wish I had thanked Jeep for being a role model. I sincerely appreciated his positive example. I made a conscious choice to ensure my sons knew, consciously and unconsciously, that they were the apple of my eye. This is an important thread that is woven into my being.

Life lesson: We never really know who is watching. We are all connected and inner-connected. A principle of Buddhism is that this interconnectedness is how we all develop. We are all related to everyone else. So when we ignore the person standing on the corner of a freeway exit with a sign asking for some money, we are ignoring a part of our own humanity.

Every human being needs to believe there is at least one other human who is absolutely crazy about them, and when a child is fortunate to have both parents, grandparents, and aunts and uncles who are crazy about them, so much the better. In an older research study of a variety of home environments, ranging from dysfunctional to almost ideal, they concluded the following. Even in the troubled homes of individuals where the children had turned out to be very successful and even exceptional as adults, those individuals could remember at least one adult in their early lives who always seemed to really like them: a teacher who frequently took the time to welcome them to class or wish them well when they left; who commented on how glad they were to see them; that they liked the student's shirt.[5] These comments of recognition were important beyond the actual grades they got on assignments and tests; these caring adults included a youth leader, a coach, an uncle, an aunt, and so on. This kind of connection contains ultimate power.

In another well-known longitudinal study on the Garden Island of Kauai, Hawaii, two-thirds of children in the study that had experienced four or more significant risk factors (anoxia at birth, death of a parent, born into alcoholic families) by age two had developed learning or behavior problems by age ten, or had delinquency records and/or mental health problems by age eighteen. However, one out of three grew into competent, confident, and caring adults. These children, who had thrived despite the significant hurdles in their lives, reported protective factors in their development: a close bond with at least one competent, emotionally stable person who was sensitive to their needs. Often this nurturing came from a substitute caregiver—grandparent, aunt, uncle, older sibling. Further, these resilient children were particularly adept at recruiting this kind of support on their own—think youth leader at church, coach, and so on. By the time these individuals reached midlife, the majority had no negative coping skills. The protective factors woven throughout the

---

5. Goertzel, Victor, & Goertzel, Mildred, (1962) *Cradles of Eminence,* Little Brown

interconnectedness of their lives, which transcended ethnic and social class boundaries, were more crucial than the adversity they had experienced.[6]

As in Thailand, I was good at my job at Minot and received the Airman of the Month Award for one of the largest Strategic Air Command (SAC) bases in the U.S. We received some gift certificates from businesses in Minot, a weekend in a hotel in Minot complete with dinners and movie tickets. We also had the use of a new car for a month. Pretty cool.

We weathered (pun intended) our time in Minot. Around this time, the Air Force was experiencing a short supply of Experienced ECM technicians. So, they were offering promotions and a bonus equal to a year's pay if we would re-enlist. It wasn't even tempting! I knew I'd be on the next deployment back to Southeast Asia. So, on June 22, 1971, we headed out the gate to the highway, with Joyce driving a packed car, Scott in a car seat next to her, and me driving an old pickup truck I had bought. The old truck was loaded with the precious earthly goods we didn't want to trust to the movers. We were going home.

The actual work I did in the Air Force was enjoyable. I liked the troubleshooting of electrical problems in the equipment and on the aircraft. But I didn't like the military part of the job. My time in the Air Force in the Vietnam War continues to take its toll on me. Besides being deaf and my occasional symptoms of PTSD, in February 2022, I was diagnosed with prostate cancer, which has been determined to result from exposure to Agent Orange. The six weeks of daily radiation and five months of hormone therapy seem to have taken care of the cancer. There are residual effects of the cancer as well as the treatment, but we caught it soon enough that I'm expected to live to an even riper old age. I've been told by different people in the VA that some of my skin cancers and my early onset of glaucoma are also likely a result of that chemical-defoliant exposure.[7] Our base in Thailand served as a storage facility for toxic defoliants, which they sprayed around the perimeter at regular intervals. Aircrews

---

6. Focal Point Research, *Policy, and Practice In Children's Mental Health,* Summer 2005, Vol 19, No 1, pages 11-14

7. Just the last couple of weeks a news article appeared in a veterans' paper that the VA now requires that all veterans seen in VA facilities be given a toxic screen and skin be examined for possible cancers.

would often have barbecues on the flight line when pilots would return from bombing missions. They used fifty-gallon metal drums, which were cut in half, to cook on. It was not uncommon to smell the meat cooking and see the smoke in the air. This is just a guess, but I suspect at least some of these metal drums had contained Agent Orange before becoming barbecue pits and setting fires in them, sending smoke into the air.

I will talk later in more detail about the Christian connections that were very important to me as I coped with being an airman in Southeast Asia during the Vietnam Conflict. It's only been in the last few decades that it has been acceptable to call Vietnam a War. Congress and the Johnson and McNamara Administration of the 60s would not call it a war because they would have had to pay their military more. By calling it only a conflict, it was also easier to cook the books, to move money around to finance a conflict rather than a declared war. (Think Kissinger's ordering three thousand plus bombings of Cambodia during the Nixon administration without Congress being aware it was going on.) Plus, a 'conflict' didn't sound as bad to them. Of course, eventually, the U.S. public got tired of the charade, which was killing over 58,000, and counting, of our young men and some 200,000 Vietnamese. Thus, the Vietnam Conflict protests of the late sixties and early seventies.

PART 3

chapter 5

New Threads

Picking up after Vietnam

The first order of business when we got back to Tacoma was to let the hair grow and enjoy being back in the mountains of Washington. In North Dakota, we did what we could to enjoy the area. We camped during the summer, but it wasn't like the Cascade Mountains in Washington. While driving across Eastern Washington, we both got tears in our eyes when we first saw the mountains.

I got a summer job working in a local paint factory in Tacoma, enrolled in college for the fall and spring semesters, and worked at a hi-fi and stereo shop evenings and weekends during the winter. We rented a townhouse a couple of miles from Pacific Lutheran University and within a bike ride of my winter job selling hi-fi and stereos.

Joyce got pregnant in the fall. Because we had just gotten out of the military, our health insurance had a twelve-month waiting period before it would pay for pregnancy. This meant it wouldn't be in effect until June 1st. Joyce was due in early June. Since she had been two weeks late with Scott, we figured we were in safe territory. Matt was born at 9:13 p.m. on May 31st.

Doug and Scott Hiking in the Cascades

The total bill came to the same amount we had saved from my work in the paint factory for my tuition the following fall. We couldn't believe it. Well, actually, we could. Fortunately, my dear Grandmother Palin loaned us the tuition money for the next academic year. My job at the hi-fi store paid only a minimal wage, so things were really tight financially. We would put cash that we had budgeted for gas in an envelope. When we had spent all the gas money, we didn't go anywhere until the next payday. Riding my bike to school and work was not for exercise; it was a necessity. We finally swallowed our pride and applied for food stamps. When the lady at the food stamp office looked at our application, she said, with some surprise, "You don't have enough money for any food." I said, "We know; that's why we're here." We told our parents that we were on food stamps. Joyce's dad said that he had been paying into the system for many years, so we're just benefitting from what he had deposited. Once you get out of college, you'll start working and pay back into the system multiple times what you are using now.

We both remember the first time we went through the checkout line at the Piggly Wiggly grocery store. We bought meat, chicken, hamburger and nearly shed tears. Since that time, when friends and family have told us they needed to get Medicaid to get medical care or go to the local food bank, I imagine it's easy to guess what we tell them. Yep, we've paid into the system, so you can draw it out, and you'll pay it back soon enough.[1] I graduated in May 1973 with a degree in Corrective Therapy.

Digging up Southern Baptist Roots and pulling threads out of the old tapestry.

When I went off to college at 19, I began gradually adding various additional aspects to my faith, as well as leaving some things behind. In today's vernacular, I guess it's referred to as deconstruction. This latest shift begun in Thailand during Vietnam, under the care of Nina Miller and while watching Buddhist monks. There is a Buddhist koan, or parable, that is applicable here. *A man builds a raft out of reeds, grasses, branches, and so on. He uses the raft to sail across a vast expanse of the river to reach the other side. He felt safe on the raft and was grateful to have it. However, once he lands on the other side, he has a choice to make. Appreciating how much the raft meant to him, he could carry the cumbersome, water-slogged, and heavy raft he used to get him to his new destination. Or, reasoning that he no longer needs it, can leave it behind on the shore. Someone else may even find it helpful.*

The water represents suffering and the trials of life. The other shore represents enlightenment. Once he arrived, he no longer needed the raft, and it would be a foolish burden to carry it on his shoulders. So he leaves it behind.

What I took with me from Southern Baptist-ism was a fairly embedded knowledge of the Bible. This was aided by the Sword Drills, of course, and the points we got each week from reporting that we read our Bible daily. Over the years, I've found this Bible knowledge to be almost second nature. I see this as a positive thing. Even now, I usually read something in the morning that has a spiritual bent. Lately, this reading has focused on Buddhism's influence on Christianity. This is also when I do my Buddhist meditation. For me, this is a good practice with which to start the day.

---

1. *Approximately half the people on welfare leave within a year; 70 percent within two years, and almost 90 percent within five years.*

Psychologically, when making changes, we usually first become dissatisfied with what we presently are doing—whether it's changing from one group to another, changing an undesirable habit, a thought pattern, or an attitude. Sometimes, we're confronted with a better alternative that gets our attention. Or we just become dissatisfied. When early changes have come about in my faith, it has been the result of seeing some incongruities in what I believed, seeing a better alternative, or both. This usually starts gradually and, over time, becomes more conscious, developing into a plan, of sorts, for change. Emotionally and psychologically in this phase, we may appear to be grumpy or edgy, malcontent, and even curmudgeonly. However, the process works for each person, at some point, we make a break with the past. Then, once we've moved away, we find ourselves in a second phase. We begin to relax and become comfortable being gone. Once we've left in our mind, we often find a new thing to take the old one's place. We may actually leave physically or only in our minds. We sometimes join something new rather quickly, or we may search for new options for quite a while. If we are changing behaviors, smaller steps toward a new habit usually work better. For me, the changes have often been brewing in my mind for some time. It's almost like I need to build a case before I jump.

However once we recognize the need for change, it becomes possible to change, sometimes in small steps and sometimes all at once, cold turkey. Often, the biggest stress we experience comes from the anticipation of what's ahead because we're not totally sure exactly how this is going to go. Then once we make the jump, we experience a sense of relief. Just in the actual leaving, some of the ambiguity resolves. Leaving what is known is stressful. There is actually an entire body of research dating back 60 years or more on how people and organizations change. My first introduction to clinical psychology work, which I will discuss in more detail later, was in a Behavioral Change and Teaching Clinic in the VA.

How important it actually is for us to understand how we got to the point where change is necessary varies for each person. An explanation for what is going on is dependent, in part, on which psychological theory you hold to. Here's my view. Maybe as a motivator to make change and to see what we can learn from the past, understanding how we got to where we are is necessary. But to actually make a change, understanding all the past isn't really that important. Granted, it may make for an interesting talk at a party. But if an in-depth understanding of the past is important, it very often comes along after the fact—with hindsight. Paradoxically, once we gain an understanding of this, this understanding is then no longer necessary. Trying to cling to this understanding can interfere with change when we cling too tightly to trying to understand more and more deeply.

What I've just said about individual change is, with some variations, true for human organizations and systems as well—be they political, religious, or social. Again, understanding the past may help to understand the present— functional and dysfunctional—and for setting goals for change. But at some point, a break is necessary, and stepping into the present is necessary. Clinging too tightly to this understanding and trying to deepen our knowledge can actually get in the way. It can immobilize us and be a source of emotional pain.

An old saying comes to mind about the 'paralysis of self-analysis'. Once we clearly understand that where we are at present is not where we want to be, we can change. Being disenchanted with the present is the motivation to change. Martin Luther would not have nailed his 95 theses to the Wittenberg Castle Door if he had not been dissatisfied with Catholicism. John Wesley's message came on the heels of dissatisfaction with Calvin's hardline approach and the doctrine of predestination; Calvin, known as the "Conscience of Geneva," *was part of birthing the Reformation. None of these intended to establish a new religion per se or a new Christian denomination. But they stood on the shoulders of those who had gone before them.*

So, from my religious experiences in Thailand and Joyce's childhood roots in the Pentecostal church, we found ourselves drawn to a rather unorthodox, for the time, Christian fellowship—the Saturday Night Meeting—closely paralleling the Jesus People movement of the late '60s and '70s. Eventually, many of the Jesus People groups either went by the wayside or got absorbed into established Christian denominations. Henry Nouwen has said that the Jesus People charismatic movement was a valid religious movement, but it lacked specific structures or frameworks to sustain itself.[2]

---

2. *Henri Nouwen (1932-1996) was a Dutch Catholic priest, professor, author and theologian. His interests were rooted in psychology, pastoral ministry, spirituality, social justice and community.*

When we first got back to Tacoma, we tried some Southern Baptist churches. But since my last name was Henning, it was suggested that we might be happier somewhere else. Apparently, while we had been away in the military, the religious landscape had shifted on the West Coast and in the Pacific Northwest. My cousin Brad, along with my two sisters, was meeting with some college students and some Jesus People. By the time we got home, as Brad had emerged as the group's leader, Brad Henning's name was persona non grata with many conservative established churches. He was associated with those hippies, sometimes referred to as Jesus freaks. The Saturday Night Meeting had grown to about two hundred young people. Conservative Christian churches, like Southern Baptist churches, were concerned that their young people would be attracted to this movement. The word was that some churches and parents would rather have had their kids into drugs rather than be associated with the Jesus freaks. The Saturday Night Meeting would continue into the early 1980s, with attendance around seven to eight hundred.

So the churches we visited didn't want anyone named Henning. We were being rejected by our old group, which we were happy to leave. We began attending the Saturday Night Meeting with a bunch of hippies and students. They had moved from my parent's house to meeting in a small church that allowed them to meet on Saturday nights. The only condition was that they wear shoes, so the oils and dirt from their feet wouldn't stain the carpet.

Major religions of the world and significant shifts within those religions have been birthed over the last many centuries. Gautama, seeking to reach beyond the Hinduism of the time, became the seeker who eventually experienced enlightenment while sitting under the Bodhi Tree and became the Buddha. His teachings led to Buddhism. Buddha's purpose of teaching was to "remove the arrows of suffering," not to establish a competing religion with Hinduism. He was not a Buddhist. He saw himself as a teacher. Although Buddhism is presently viewed and experienced as a religion, a form of spirituality, it did not start that way. The roots of Buddhism are more of a philosophy. Buddha did not believe that he was some kind of savior, nor did he believe in God. He was a wisdom teacher.

Jesus was not intent on establishing Christianity as a major religion. He was not a Christian. He was a teacher who saw the need to address problems in Judaism so that the spirit of God would be evident among them, as a people. So Jesus stood on the shoulders, so to speak, of the Judaism he was born into as he attempted to point out Judaism's flaws. He sought to make Judaism's beliefs and practices more consistent with his understanding of the Spirit of God. Buddhism, which spread from India to the north and west, probably influenced Jesus. Over the last several years, I've come to believe that Jesus picked up where Buddha had left off. My understanding is that Buddha, like Jesus, did not intend to establish a new religion. He laid out and taught a moral and kinder way of relating to others and to ourselves, and to remove suffering.

chapter 6

Threads of The VA

COLLEGE II

I graduated with my bachelor's degree in Corrective Therapy (CT) from Pacific Lutheran University in 1973. CT was similar to physical therapy in the VA hospital systems. I intended to work a while as a CT, to take a break from school, and reduce the stress on us as a family from the pressures of college and the financial burden of scrimping by. I fully intended to return to college and earn a degree in physical therapy, which would give me greater professional flexibility. I had done an internship in CT at American Lake Veterans Hospital in Tacoma before graduating. When I graduated, there were no openings for CTs at the VA, so I went back to work at the paint factory, canning paint and climbing down inside two-thousand-gallon vats to clean them for the next batch of paint.

Over the few years I worked at Parker Paint, Joyce would tell me that my breath smelled like paint and lacquer thinner. This was before OSHA[1], so the only ventilation in the factory was opening the windows when it was warm enough to do so. Joyce kept telling me she was praying,

---

1. The Occupational Safety and Health Administration

and she believed that an opening in CT at the VA would come up, so we wouldn't have to move. I humored her.

Just as my summer job in the paint factory was ending, I got a call from the head of Corrective Therapy at American Lake. A Corrective Therapist had unexpectedly resigned to move to another part of the country. He wanted to know if I was interested in applying for the job. I was, I did, and I got the job. Joyce has always had a spiritual sense about her, of which confidence, tenderness, and kindness are hallmarks. So I started at American Lake in October 1973.

American Lake VA Medical Center is a neuropsychiatric facility with a blind rehabilitation clinic, alcohol/substance abuse program, nursing home unit, and traditional medical units. It also had a large psychology department and twenty-five-plus psychologists, several of whom served as role models for me. In short order, I got to know a psychologist who

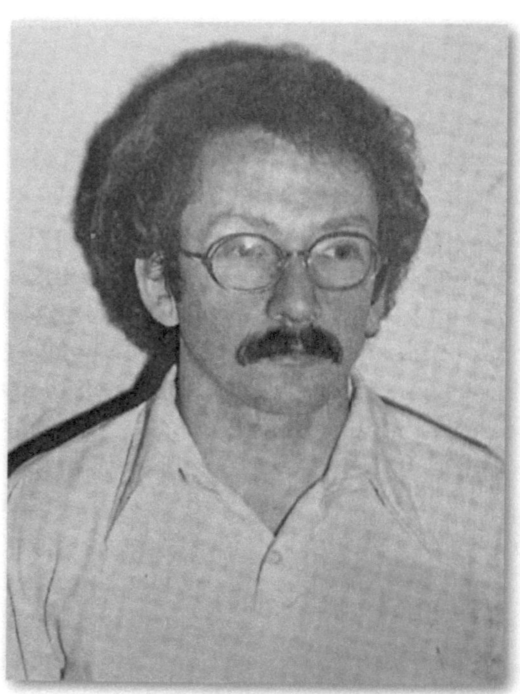

Corrective Therapist in VA

worked closely with the medical inpatient and outpatient programs. The psychologist, Dr. Willard (Will) Snow, had an office just down the hall from my CT clinic. My minor for my bachelor's degree was psychology. The more I got to know Will, the more intrigued I became with the behaviorism used in treating problematic medical, psychological, and behavioral issues. I began working closely with Will in his Behavioral Teaching clinic on some cases, and before long, I was hooked. Even though I continued working as a CT, I began pursuing my master's degree in psychology in the evenings and on weekends. About two-and-a-half years later, I took a position as a psychology technician and worked directly with Will. I also began working in the Blind Rehabilitation Clinic as a psychologist. These exposures to the application of psychology to medicine and rehabilitation turned out to be rich experiences for me. They shaped me as a psychologist and an adult. As I've looked back over my career in psychology, I've realized how fortunate I've been to be in the right place at the right time. It feels like these right-places-at-the-right-times were providential.

My responsibilities in the Psychology Department included doing psychological assessments for the general hospital population and for the Blind Clinic and Substance Abuse residents. Because of the patient's blindness, I had to adapt the assessment process for Blind Clinic Residents. This was a pretty creative process, which I really enjoyed. Also, working closely with Dr. Snow in the Behavioral Teaching Clinic was a tremendous bonus. He was trained in Chronic Pain Behavioral Management at the University of Washington. This was a new area and considered cutting-edge.

An aspect of Pain Management was employing biofeedback technology. Our clinic, apart from university and research facilities, was the first clinic of its kind on the West Coast. This was fun and enjoyable work. In short, Biofeedback is a method of measuring very subtle neurological, physiological, and physical responses with sensitive electronic equipment. Surface electrodes are placed on the skin over the problem area, and the patient is provided with the information. The patient can then use the feedback to learn how to control various physical functions. The physical symptoms, usually thought to be automatic responses, were muscle tension, skin temperature, galvanic skin responses, and others. These various areas are often involved in natural responses to stress, as well as specific diseases such as tension and migraine headaches, Raynaud's disease, and high blood pressure, to name a few.

Early on, we were pretty sure Biofeedback was close to a cure-all. The fun part for us was that we would get patients who had tried many other methods, including medication, with no or little improvement. One nurse who worked at American Lake that I remember came to us with severe migraine headaches. She was missing so much work that she was in jeopardy of losing her job. The side effects of the medication used for some patients were almost as bad as the headaches themselves. After a few weeks of biofeedback, temperature, and muscle tension therapy, she had diminished her use of medication significantly and missed no work for over a month.

We rarely turned anyone away. A young man in his twenties was referred by his primary care physician at the VA. He had a severe stuttering problem. He was an EMT, but when he got stressed by an emergency he had responded to, his stutter made it all but impossible for him to talk on the radio. He told me he had been prayed for numerous times at his conservative Christian church without any improvement. Even though his mom was very skeptical of psychology, he was desperate and wanted to try. Because of my personal history of stuttering, I was well aware of how much stress and anxiety made the stutter worse.

I told Dr. Snow I thought if we placed the surface electrodes on the front of his neck and he could learn to relax his throat muscles, he could learn to control his stutter. Bingo! He learned within a few weeks to relax his throat muscles, so the stutter became a non-issue. Interestingly, toward the end of his treatment schedule, he suddenly missed a couple of follow-up appointments. I called his home, and his mother answered. I told her who I was and asked if he was okay. She explained he had recently been prayed for at their church and was healed, so he wouldn't need to see me anymore. Although I didn't say "Praise the Lord," I did say that I was happy he was doing better and that the next time he was at the hospital, I'd like for him to stop by the clinic and say hi. I concluded that his family's fundamentalist religious beliefs would not allow them to admit that psychology had helped him gain control over his stuttering.

The field of biofeedback has expanded today to include neurofeedback, which focuses on brain activity. One example is the conscious production of brain waves, which are associated with deep relaxation and calm.

Another example of a biofeedback application was with blind patients. The Blind Rehab program was an inpatient residential program. Residents would need to learn how to get along without their sight. This included, among other things, using [white] cane techniques to get around, braille for reading, and arranging their physical environment so it's predictable. It doesn't take much imagination to realize how stressful this learning process can be. Besides being newly blind, the person finds themself in an intensive learning environment. Stress can really interfere with learning new tasks. We found that by teaching these newly blinded individuals how to reduce their stress levels through biofeedback, they could speed up their ability to learn new tasks as well as how much material they could learn a limited time period. The result was a reduction in the time they had to remain in the program by at least a month. This meant more frequent slots in the program for other patients and new patients, and better use of staff resources. I occasiionally followed a patient down the hall with the biofeedback equipment hooked to a resident's shoulders and forehead. This allowed him to get auditory feedback while using his cane so he could learn to relax as much as possible. This increased ability to relax also allowed the patient to key in more effectively to cues from their environment. Cues like subtle changes in air temperature, which would signal passing a window even when closed, or an intersecting hallway passage, as well as auditory information: traffic sounds, sounds of air conditioners that were unique to a particular room at work.

I worked at American Lake for nearly six years. The first couple of years were spent as a Corrective Therapist. Over the years, I worked for the V.A. in addition to the excellent professional experience, I learned a lot from the patients with whom I interacted. The C.T. clinic where I worked served outpatients, and the Nursing Home Unit, which was in the same building. As the name implies, the Nursing Home patients were usually older and required full-time medical as well as psychiatric care.

One patient is hard to forget. He was a grumpy old man with dementia, likely caused in part by years of alcohol abuse. His family rarely, if ever, visited him. His family essentially abandoned him. My job with him was to increase his level of physical activity. He would come to the clinic three mornings a week. Part of his routine was to ride a stationary bicycle. He grumbled the whole time. He had quite a colorful vocabulary, using swear words in ways I had rarely heard them used, even back to my days in the Air Force and working construction. This colorful language included names he would call me. My hair was quite curly, and I wore my hair in a long afro. Among other names, he would call me a G-D-F. ing hippie. I really liked this old fart and felt bad that he never had a family visit him. His lack of family visitors meant he never had any human touch other than nursing and medical staff. So, no loving or gentle physical contact.

I decided I would be the loving contact for him. This was the mid-1970s, so smoking was permitted inside buildings and offices. He was a smoker, as were many, many veterans. I began asking him if he would like a cup of coffee and a cigarette before he got started on the bike. I'd get him a cup of coffee and a cigarette and sit beside him while he smoked and drank his coffee.

After he got used to having a smoke and coffee and sitting by me, I told him I had a new set of medical orders for him. I needed to give him a shoulder massage while he was riding the stationary bike. Of course, he grumbled about this, expressing himself in typically colorful language, but agreed to let me give him a shoulder massage *so I wouldn't get in trouble. (He would use the 'F' word as a verb, noun, adverb, adjective, or part of larger compound words.)*

In short order, I could feel his shoulders relax as soon as I touched him. This went on for the entire time I worked in this clinic. From time to time, he would talk about how much he used to enjoy drinking beer after a long day working in the fields on his farm. Probably drank too much beer. One day, his doctor was in the clinic, and we were talking about how various patients were doing. I don't remember the whole conversation, but he must have mentioned how much more cooperative my foul-mouthed patient had been lately. I told him about the cigarettes, coffee, and shoulder massages. The doctor smiled and told me again that this man's family had never visited him. I mentioned how he had talked about missing having a beer. Much to my surprise, he said that if I could sneak beer into my office for him, it would be okay to let him have some. I'm sure I looked surprised. He told me we hadn't had this conversation, but a little beer wasn't going to hurt. You could buy six-ounce bottles of beer. So I bought a six-pack and hid it in my office file cabinet. One day, I told him I needed to talk to him in my office. While he grumbled, I pushed his wheelchair into my office and closed the door. I told him I had a treat for himbut that he couldn't tell anyone. I didn't worry that he would tell. His memory and his cognitive processes were confused enough that no one would believe him anyway. As he tipped back the small bottle of beer, he tipped his head back, smiled, and sighed. I can still see that expression as if it were just a short while ago. I clearly had a friend for life. While this is the only time I've ever brought alcohol into a clinic setting, the importance of human touch and kindness was brought home to me that day and continued to be reinforced throughout my career over the next fifty years.

One other patient, resident, in the Blind Clinic also stands out in my memory. These veterans were newly blinded, either from diseases like diabetes or other neurological impairments or from some Traumatic Brain Injury (TBI). This man was blind from a failed suicide attempt. He had used a gun but had only severed his optic nerve just behind his eyes. The result was that he was totally blind. These veterans were from all over the northwest part of the U.S., so their families were often not close enough for regular visits. The usual stay in the program was around nine months or longer. Part of the Blind Rehab Program was that, toward the end of the resident's stay, the clinic would bring a close family member in so they could see what the residents had learned and learn how best to support them when they went home. The clinic would put the family member up in a local motel for a week, and the resident would usually stay with them. This man's wife came to visit him. As time drew closer for his wife's visit, he talked about how much he was looking forward to being with her. It was touching to watch them together around the clinic and hospital grounds. This older couple holding hands and whispering to each other.

When his wife's visit ended, and she had gone home, I asked him how he thought the visit had gone. He said it was great, but there was one thing that surprised him and maybe disappointed him. He confided that since they had not been with each other for several months, they were looking forward to having sex, which they did the first night. Then, each subsequent night through the week, they would go to bed planning to have sex, but they would get to talking about how good it was going to be when he finally got home and the type of modifications they would need to make to the house. Then, they would invariably fall asleep. His concern was whether there was something wrong with them, and he hoped it didn't mean they didn't love each other as much as they both wanted to. I told him I had a theory about what had happened if he wanted to hear it. He did. I said it sounded like they had taken their level of intimacy to a deeper level. That being intimate in a loving relationship meant a lot more than just having sexual intercourse. He smiled and thanked me, saying this made sense to him and that he felt relieved.

Two discrete events during the nearly six years I worked at American Lake VA had a lasting impact on me. They each helped shape my future and became threads that would thread throughout my life both professionally and personally. The first one was a conversation with my Corrective Therapy supervisor, Lou Souza. I mentioned offhandedly that I was wondering if I should get some more college as in graduate school. I had already started taking one psychology course a semester in the evening to better prepare myself to work closely with the psychology department. These courses were in the master's program at Pacific Lutheran University. Initially, I wasn't really sure if I would complete the degree. I just wanted a stronger background in psychology. I was secretly hesitant to commit to finishing the degree because I wasn't sure if I was smart enough. I had some challenging courses to take if I intended to commit. One of those courses was statistics. Remember, statistics had been the last course I flunked before getting drafted. The second course was in research design, which applied the Statistics.

So I was talking to Lou in his office when I asked if he thought I should get serious about getting a graduate degree; he paused, opened a drawer on his desk, and riffled through its contents. Then Lou stopped and said, "I guess I finally threw the application away." He had filled out an application form for graduate school admission sometime before, but never sent it off. He told me that one regret he had was that he never really knew if he could have succeeded in graduate school because he never tried. I decided right then that wasn't going to be me. If I tried and failed, at least I would know I gave it my best.

The second event happened after I had moved into the psychology department. As I mentioned, the Psychology Department was large. So, the associations I had with these psychologists were rich and vibrant. To name a few of the ones who really affected me were Will Snow, Anne Ganley, Lance Harris, Bob Shea, and Chris Solberg. Besides being powerful role models, they really encouraged me to see myself as capable. The department had a weekly staff meeting, which sometimes included an in-service continuing education time. One day, we had a presentation on death and dying. A presenter came to the hospital and showed a film about the research Elizabeth Kubler-Ross had been doing on the stages of death and dying. The film was a documentary made by a man and his wife. The man, Ted Rosenthal, had acute leukemia and was dying. He had about six months to live. Rosenthal said that they had been searching for things to read about what it is like to go through the death process. However, they didn't find anything, so they decided to make their own documentary and write a book of poetry. The film and the subsequent book of philosophy and poetry are excellent.[2]

This was in the mid-1970s. A vivid takeaway for me has been a thread that stayed with me for fifty-plus years. The title of the film is "How Could I Not Be Among You." The essence: how is it possible to be alive and yet not be aware of all of the people and nature that make up life around me—in the here and now? As humans in western society, we get stuck in the past, wrapped up in our failures or successes, or we get stuck worrying about the future, what might happen tomorrow, next week, month, years down the road. Rosenthal said that as a hippie of the 1960s and 70s, his ambition in life had been to have no ambition. To be truly satisfied with today. However, he had never been able to achieve that . . . until he knew he had less than six months to live. Then, finally, he could sit out in his backyard and get lost entirely in watching a bird fly across the sky and land in a tree

____

2. Rosenthal, Ted, (1987) *How Could I Not Be Among You*

close by. Knowing he was soon to die, he quit worrying about what he was going to do in the future. All he really had was NOW. I didn't make the connection then, but this is what Buddhism brings to me now in my life.

The reason this had such a profound impact on me was that I was only five years out from the Vietnam War, so I was thinking through a lot of my priorities. I was trying to make up for lost time. I was so swamped working full-time, a half-time graduate student, father of two active young boys, a husband, we were remodeling our old house, active in our church, and singing in the choir. Some of these things were far off in the future. I came home from that seminar and told Joyce about the movie, saying I really needed to take stock of things. I needed to be sure that all those I was involved in were meaningful in the present. If I were doing any of these and several other things only for some future goal and not finding any meaning in the process, I needed to stop. If any of those things didn't make our family better today, I needed to stop. Being a husband and dad came at the top of the list and, as such, was non-negotiable. I needed to be sure I was finding meaning in those roles in the now.

We were halfway through the process of working on the house. But that didn't mean I needed to do it all. So we hired a couple of friends who were builders to help. The next big one was graduate school. If I couldn't find meaning and satisfaction in what I was doing in the present, I was going to stop. I had a good job and could be satisfied with it. If need be, I could put that off until later.

The more Joyce and I talked about all of this, the more we agreed that I was getting a lot of meaning and satisfaction from the process of being in school. I really enjoyed the "process" of learning and being in school. So, as long as that was the case, I would continue. Going to school was my hobby. But when the master's degree was done, we would put a pause on school for a while. A year after finishing the master's, at dinner one evening, Joyce said that if I could find a doctoral program that was in the Pacific Northwest, so we didn't have to move too far from family, she was willing to consider it. She had caught her breath from constant schoolwork and thought it would be fun to move if necessary for a while. Joyce would also begin renewing her teaching certificate so she could start substitute teaching to help financially.

chapter 7

Another Thread – More University Work

Following that conversation, I began investigating psychology doctoral programs in the Northwest. While I was applying to doctoral programs, The Saturday Night Meeting, which we were still attending, became an actual part of the church, which allowed the meeting to use its sanctuary—The People's Church. A year following the completion of my master's degree, because I was seriously looking for doctoral programs, I resigned from my job at the VA. I took a position at the church and began developing a community counseling center. I worked for them for seven years, including a year and a half-long leave of absence to complete the coursework for my doctoral studies.

My first choice of doctoral program was the University of Washington in Seattle. This would mean I could commute from Tacoma to Seattle, we wouldn't need to relocate, and I could work part-time in Tacoma. The head of the VA Psychology Department, Chris, had become a good friend and mentor. He encouraged me to apply to the University of Washington. The Chair of the university psychology department was a friend of his. Chris wrote me a strong letter of reference, as did Will Snow. Even though I had a solid GPA from my master's degree, because my undergraduate records were less than stellar for the first two-and-a-half years, the U of W had some concerns. The competition to get in was tough. However, they would allow me to interview for the program.

I had appointments with three of the faculty members. If I got a thumbs up from all three, they would admit me to the program. I remember two of the three faculty interviews as if they were yesterday. The third is only a vague memory for me. It was the first interview of the day, with the head of the Counseling Psychology department. That interview went fine, and the professor told me he would be happy to recommend me for acceptance. At the beginning of the second interview, Professor B began by saying he noticed I had been working part-time for a church in Tacoma. He asked if I was a Christian. When I affirmed that this was the case, he said that he didn't believe that Christians made good psychologists and, therefore, could not recommend me for acceptance into the program. But if I wanted to use the allotted time, he would be happy to talk with me. (How very generous of him. This was the late seventies, and it must have been okay to discriminate based on creed.) Needless to say, this was a huge disappointment. I knew I had to get approval from all three interviewers. I decided to go to the third interview. When I walked into Professor Bashi's office, beads hung across the door—remember, this was the 70s, and we sat on beanbags. The professor was Hindu. He seemed very kind and asked me how my first two interviews had gone. I told him about Professor B's comments and that I was really disappointed. He said he wanted to apologize for Larry and that he wished the requirement was not to have 100 percent approval. He said that what Larry didn't understand was that all of us have a faith that we go by. Larry's religion was just his psychology. So, after a few days of feeling sorry for myself, I began searching for other programs in the North West.

An ironic turn is that twenty-five years later, when I was teaching at a small Christian university in Kansas, we used Professor B's text on counselor training in our undergraduate and master's counseling programs. I told a colleague the story of my history with Dr. B. He asked me why I would use this guy's book. The answer was simple. It was well done.

After we had used the text for a few years, the publisher contacted me and asked if I would be willing endorsement for a new edition. What I wrote was printed on the front of the book. He had co-authored the latest edition with a professor and Christian at Seattle Pacific University, a private Methodist university. I knew of this professor and her husband, who was also a psychology professor at SPU. Karma. I don't imagine Professor B never made the connection that the professor who had endorsed his book was the applicant he had denied admission was now a college professor, chair of the psychology department, and a licensed psychologist. Additionally, his co-author was a Christian and a psychologist. All of this felt like karma just the same.

COLLEGE III

A year following my disappointment at the U of W, I got into Oregon State University (OSU) in Corvallis, Oregon. One reason I was pleased to get into OSU was that they used their doctoral students to teach and supervise students in their Master's in Counseling program. I saw this as an opportunity to hone my teaching skills.

Since I was going to be doing my doctoral studies, which was a dream come true, this time should be fun for our boys as well. Scott had always been smitten with horses and would save his allowance money to go riding at a small riding stable not too far from our house in Parkland, Washington.

So we drove to OSU before we moved so we could see what housing was going to be like. I looked into the possibility of renting a faculty member's house while they are on sabbatical. Bingo! A professor in the agricultural chemistry department was going to Australia for a year. He had a five-acre mini ranch with a barn and five head of cattle.

We rented his mini-ranch and bought one of the steers to finish raising it. Then, we had it butchered, so we had a supply of beef. We looked around and bought a horse. We were ranchers! Remember, the only things we knew about horses were what Scott, twelve years old, had read. Our horse was white, three-quarters Arab. Her name was Snow Fire, which should have tipped us off to her personality. The lady who sold us Snow Fire, sensing how much we were true greenhorns, offered to come to our place for a while and give Scott riding lessons at no charge. Even with the riding lessons, the horse turned out to be too much horse for Scott and, by extension, for me. After a few months, we started looking around to sell her and then planned to buy another one that was more our speed. At first the only offers we got for Snow Fire were from people we sensed were going to slaughter her for glue and dog food. We weren't doing that. Then, out of the blue, we got a call from a student at OSU who wanted to know if we were interested in trading Snow Fire for a horse she had that was Welsh and Quarter—Tekla. The student had had Tekla since she was in grade school and had gone through 4-H with her. She was gentle and good with inexperienced riders. So we made the trade. I had become a horse trader. (I never quite figured out where to put this on my resume.)

In addition to being a horse trader, Scott and I became conversant regarding the nutritional quality of various types of hay. For instance, Timothy Hay, which grows in western Oregon, is fine as a filler, but doesn't have near the protein content that Alfalfa (16 percent protein) has, which is grown east of the mountains. So we had to buy Alfalfa hay to supplement Tekla's and the steer's diet. We also learned that tansy ragwort weed is poisonous to livestock. All we really knew was that the weed had a yellow flower and grew in pastures. So we were on the lookout! We had pictures in books, but we worried about it to the point of paranoia. On several occasions, I would dig up a yellow-looking weed and take it to the local feed store to ask if *this* was tansy. It got so that as soon as I'd walk through the feed store door, the guy behind the counter would say "NO" before I could even ask. To my recollection, we never did find tansy. This hunt for tansy almost had the feel of a snipe hunt during Boy Scout camp.

More Adventures in Novice Ranching

The entire experience of renting a five-acre mini-ranch was a fun and educational experience for all of us. So we decided to continue our gentleman farming venture when we returned to Washington. We sold our 80-year-old house in Parkland and found a house in Puyallup that had two acres with a loafing shed. Tekla had a new home. We eventually bought three additional acres adjacent to the loafing shed. I had noticed an old barn that was falling apart and approached the owner about having the wood. The lady's husband had passed away a few years prior. She told me that some neighbors had complained about the barn being dangerous for kids to play in. So, if I would be sure to haul away everything, I could have the barn. Joyce, the boys, and I took the barn apart board by board and hauled the material about a half mile to our place. Over the summer we built a pole barn which took in the loafing shed. This doubled the size of the shed which gave us two more stalls, a grain room and a loft which held three tons of hay.

So now we had a modest little barn and a few acres. We learned of a dairy about 15 miles south of us that often sold bull calves during calving season, when they were 3 to 5 days old. As long as we lived on our little ranch, about every fifteen months we would go out to the dairy and buy a couple bull calves that Matt and Scott raised. They sold sides of beef to our friends, bought new baby calves with the profits, and pocketed a few hundred dollars.

The Dairy Farmer we bought the calves from stressed that these new babies were fragile and needed tender, loving care for the first few weeks. So we would go out to the dairy for the first couple of months and buy milk to feed them with a bottle and nipple. We gradually weaned them from the dairy milk to a fortified formula. Feeding them from the bottles was fun and cute. By instinct, when feeding from mama, the calf will butt the udder to stimulate the milk flow. So when they thought the milk wasn't coming fast enough from the bottle, they would butt the bottle. While this was cute when they were only a few weeks old, as they got bigger, if we weren't prepared, they could knock us over. Even after they had been weaned from the milk, because these calves got pretty tame as they got bigger, they would follow us around the barn yard and from time to time would come up to us and give us a friendly head butt. We only had one calf over the ten years that we were afraid might not make it. He didn't seem to be strong enough to nurse from the bottle. So every morning before I would go to the office, I went out with a couple of bottles of formula, sat in the stall with this baby's head in my lap, and massaged his neck to help him swallow. He eventually began to thrive and got as strong as the other calf.

Although I liked to say we were "ranchers," in fact we were truly novices, which meant much of what we learned and did came from talking to feed store salespeople, and from innovations learned by trial and error. We were hobby ranchers and treated our steers and Tekla like pets. Tekla would often hear the garage door open when one of us was heading out to work, so she would trot to the gate and wait for her treat. Her treat was a slice of toast with peanut butter. We'd place the peanut butter side on her tongue.and she would eat and lick her lips while we patted her nose.

Errors that we made were usually not that big of a deal with relatively easy and straightforward solutions, often with a mixture of humor and occasionally some pain. Scott joined the FFA at school. This meant we needed an FFA project, like a steer, with the goal of taking it to the state fair. The bull calves we got from the dairy didn't qualify because they were not purebred beef cattle. So, early one Saturday, Scott, along with some other FFA students and their teacher, drove to Eastern Washington to buy show-quality Hereford steers. These steers had been on the open range, meaning they had not been confined to fences or stalls. They were the epitome of a Wild March Hare.

One morning, shortly after bringing this wild steer home, as I was driving out the driveway on my way to the office, I saw the new steer standing in the middle of a neighbor's garden. The lady was yelling and waving a dish towel in the air, with her little dog running around yipping at the steer. I was in my good clothes. The steer had run through our fence and crossed the road. The yelling lady, towel waving at the steer, and the yipping dog was clearly not helping calm the animal. I jumped out of the car and ran across the road. The lady started yelling at me, which didn't help me either, but I just thought this wasn't the time to try to explain it to her. I somehow headed the steer back down our driveway, into the pasture, and into one of the stalls. I'm sure I briefly considered how I could hurt this 450-pound animal, or perhaps even getting the 22 rifle and slaughtering it right then and there. But this was Scott's FFA project, and he had already given it a name—BIG MAC, named after the McDonald's sandwich. I closed the stall gate and nailed an extra layer of old boards across it. I went into the house and kicked off my shoes in the garage, which had quite a bit of horse and cow manure by them. I changed my clothes and headed to work.

The solution was to tame this animal down ASAP, reinforce the fencing, and run an electric fence around the perimeter of the pasture. Scott had been reading and talking to his FFA instructor about how to tame a range steer.[1] Actually, within about ten days, Scott had calmed Bid Mac down considerably, the fence was reinforced and electrified.

ECT *(electroconvulsive shock therapy)*

There were times when we needed to keep the steers and horses separate—we had acquired one more horse along the way. We had an old bathtub to use as a water trough and placed it parallel to the water faucet and hose on the side of the barn. So we wouldn't have to get a second water trough, we built a gate that would straddle the trough, so the animals could get to the trough from both pastures. The problem was that as the calves bulked up, around 900 pounds by butchering time, they would lean on the gate and break it open. So, necessity being the mother of invention, I stretched an electric fence parallel to the gate across the trough. This worked really well—horses on one side in their pasture and steers on the other. Since the horses learned to be wary of any fence that may be electrified, I only needed the electric fence on the side the steers used. Steers just weren't that smart and would forget about the electrified fence. I was pretty proud of this barnyard innovation, until I wasn't.

During cold snaps, the water would freeze on top of the trough.,so one of us would need to go out and break the ice in the mornings. We kept a brick beside the barn to break the ice. I went out one Sunday morning before heading to church to break the ice. After breaking the ice, I needed to reach in and get the brick so it would be ready for the next morning. The brick had fallen toward the middle just under the gate. As I was reaching for the brick, my forehead touched the electric fence, and my hand was in the water. BAM! Knocked me back so that I stood up real quick and stumbled backwards on my fanny in the dirt. As with

---

1. Range Steers are cattle who have been running wild on the open range. So they are not used to being confined.

trial-and-error learning experiencers of this magnitude, this turned out to be a one-time learning experience for me. I didn't need to go over this lesson a second time. I had a red line across my forehead for a few days and joked that my depression was all better—ECT (electroconvulsive shock therapy). I guess I wasn't any smarter than the steers.

When we returned to Washington, from Oregon, I had gone back to work at People's Church to expand the counseling service. I started working on my dissertation over next eighteen months. This was a hectic time for me—working full time, gathering the data for and writing my dissertation, and being a husband and father. Joyce decided to return to full-time teaching and got a job at the private school associated with the People's Church.

OUR DEVELOPING SELF (It seems to me)

During my doctoral work at Oregon State, I developed a strong sense of developmentalism: that as humans, we become who we are rather than being born as we are. While we are born with genetic tendencies, the outcomes depend, in large part, on cultural factors, family environment, social- economic-factors, and so on. These are what shape us. Who we are at present is the cumulative impact of our past experiences, accomplishments, and failures, as well as the various roles we have taken on. This is good news because our development is a malleable process; we are not stuck or doomed to who we are, as we would be if we were born to be who we are for our whole lives.

In more common vernacular, we stand on the shoulders of those experiences and people we've interacted with in the past. When gaining an understanding of who we are, it's impossible to separate the impact of the past from the present. So, to have an understanding of who a person is, it helps to understand the social norms, cultural values, and so forth that brought them to the present. It helps to understand the past that has brought us to now. Further, we continue to become throughout our whole life. We are always developing/becoming, never static. So, who we are tomorrow and next week will be at least somewhat different from who we are today. A permanent self does not exist. Looking back, I realize this was a follow-up from my master's degree work on Buddhist philosophy. I didn't recognize it as such at the time. It just seemed like good Cognitive Behavior Psychology. These and other Buddhist principles fit well with good psychology because, as I've realized in recent years, that's where it came from. Who and what we are now is all we have. The past is gone, the old has passed away, and the new is always being birthed.[2] The thing we always have control over is how we view a situation. Perception is often everything.

In the field of psychological assessment and testing, a formal assessment loses its validity after some time, often within some months, because our personality, at least the expression of it, is always developing. Clearly, there are noticeable benchmarks of change as we take on and leave off various roles: child, student, boyfriend, girlfriend, employee, spouse, parent, and grandparent. As the process of changing roles continues, we often become caretakers or parents of our parents while we become grandparents and retirees. We are never static.

---

2. 2 Corinthians 5:17

PART 4

chapter 8

Professional Psychologist

Getting Licensed

I graduated from OSU in 1983. Next, I began studying for my psychology licensing exam. There is a national written exam that most states use, but each state's psychology licensing board sets the passing score. Washington and a couple of other states had the highest cutoff score—75%. In other states, the cutoffs were sixty-five to seventy percent. I took the exam and got 70%. I knew I needed to retake it. I had never really learned how to take a good multiple-choice exam. So I chalked it up to that, because I was confident in what I knew. Professors would tell me that based on my questions and comments in class and conversations with them, it was obvious that I knew more than my test scores usually indicated.

An interesting aside: Attached to the letter I received telling me I had not passed the exam was a note from the exam administrator. It said that the reason it had taken a little longer for me to get the results was that there had been some confusion between my score and a Mr. Hanson's. We had been seated in the exam room in alphabetical order, so I had sat next to Hanson. Somehow, our two answer sheets had gotten mixed up, and they couldn't tell which was which. So, through some process, that wasn't clear, they assigned the passing score to Hanson and the failing score to me. What?? I had thought that I had done pretty well on the exam. Had I had the confidence then that I later acquired when getting licensed in Kansas, I would have submitted a formal protest. (An explanation of the Kansas drama is later.) Nonetheless, here I was.

Years before this, I had graduated with my bachelor's degree and was in the middle of a Master's program, was working full time for the VA, active in my church, a husband and father of two active sons, and remodeling our old house to meet our needs for more space. One morning, I was reading the Old Testament in the book of Ezekiel. I was struggling to juggle all of my responsibilities and wondering why some things didn't come more easily to me.

I came across a scriptural text that jumped out at me. The metaphor is of the *River of Life, which was flowing from the Temple.*[1] This river would produce fish of all kinds, similar to the great sea, and would be in abundance. Everything this river touched became fresh. It is the source of life. Trees and plants growing on its banks will produce food, and their *leaves will be used for healing. In short, this river is the source of life.* Then, verse eleven: But its swamps and marshes will not become fresh; they will be left for salt. Salt? Salt is a preservative. It prevents rotting, enhances taste, cleanses, and promotes healing. Salt is an essential element of life itself.

Whenever I've been hiking and fishing along mountain streams, I've avoided stepping in swamps and marshes—they stink and are slimy. The bottoms are mushy and easy to get bogged down in. But according to this metaphor, they will not be the pure water that the rest of the river of life is.

Biologists have told me that swamps and marshes, which are found along the edges of rivers and streams, act as filters, collecting debris from the main flow of the rest of the river. This is often what, our struggles in life are, they're filters and salt. As the saying goes, since they do not kill us, their purpose is to make us stronger. Stronger so we can cope with more struggles that come our way in the future. Buddhism tells us that pain and struggle are just a fact of life. They're one of the four foundational truths. As we get better at dealing

---

1. *Ezekiel 47:8-12*

with hard times, we learn not to let them sidetrack us, because they are only temporary.

The last couple of years at Peoples', it became apparent that it was time to leave. The lack of support for a community-based counseling center was one of the motivating factors. It was not financially profitable for the church. Even at the start of working there, I was aware that, as a charismatic church, they didn't see a counseling center as a primary focus of the church's ministry and goals. But I had sold them on the need for counseling in the community. I believed then, as I do now, that the church should take responsibility and be available to meet the social, emotional, and psychological needs of the people living in the community around them, especially when those people are not members. At the time, many conservative Christians still thought that if you prayed enough, counseling and psychology were unnecessary to cope with normal everyday human problems (i.e., divorce, forced early retirement, parent-child conflict, neurochemical conditions like anxiety, depression, personality issues like bipolar disorder and obsessive-compulsive disorders, etc.) Going to a psychologist or counselor was seen as a sign of a lack of faith. It was as if seeking psychological help actually prevented spiritual growth.

In actuality, research is pretty clear that the treatment of choice for disorders associated with neurochemical issues is usually a combination of medication and counseling. These conditions result from being human, not from sin. Even though this has softened somewhat in the last decades, it is still prevalent, especially among more conservative Christian denominations. But I naively hoped that, over time, having a counseling center open to the surrounding community might take a more central place in its ministry. That did not happen. A few years following my resignation, the counselor who moved into my position died suddenly. To my knowledge, they did not replace him.

The salary from People's Church, while I was there, was lower than what I needed to make ends meet. We actually qualified for food from the Tacoma food bank, as did others who were on staff then. Even so, I was sure that working there was where I was supposed to be. In an effort to make ends meetI, I decided to do some extra work. So in 1984, with the Senior Pastors' approval, as long as I juggled my schedule to get in my 40 hours a week at the church, I began working a day a week with a Family Physician at a medical center in Tacoma. This provided a little more income, needed to make ends meet for our family with two teenage boys and school loans. Consistent with the epiphany at the VA I had on the tail end of the seminar on death and dying, I needed to structure this additional work so it didn't distract from Joyce and the boys.

Back in my VA days, working in the Psychology Department, the chief of the psychology department, who was a Christian, told me that I had a good balance of not letting spirituality influence my psychological knowledge. Following the completion of my master's degree in psychology, and before attending OSU, I applied for an internship in the Sexual Dysfunction Clinic at the University of Washington in Seattle. It was 1979. The importance of my personal religiousness came up. I must have had something in my application form that tipped off one of the co-directors, a psychiatrist, that religion was important to me. I don't remember the question he asked or my response, but the other co-director told me later that the psychiatrist had said, when I left the interview, that I was a religious-type he could understand work with, and like.

Even though I apparently had a "good balance" and didn't let my spirituality interfere with my psychology, and vice versa, I often felt like I could not tell the entire story of what I really believed to fellow Christians or fellow psychologists. On the rare occasion that I mentioned my true beliefs to Christian friends and colleagues, they responded that my liberal education and experience had too much of an influence on me. I have realized that the cognitive dissonance I sometimes experienced in those early years was because of my very conservative multigenerational Christian roots. I have since disavowed myself from conservative evangelical Christianity. This has been a gradual process over the last fifty-plus years.

So when I decided it was time for me to leave Peoples', in 1986, in addition to my one day a week with the Family Physician, I had the good fortune of getting a supervised Rehabilitation Psychology position at Good Samaritan Rehabilitation Hospital in Puyallup, three days per week. This was a dream job for me in that it gave me the opportunity to merge my earlier career in Corrective Therapy and psychology. Since I had not yet passed the psychology licensing exam, a condition of my continued employment was that I pass it. I took the exam again. This time, missing the cutoff by one question, 74.5 percent. No rounding up.

Shortly after missing the passing score by .5 percent, I was standing in the office at Good Samaritan and looking out the window. The hospital sat on a hill facing northwest. It was a rare, very clear fall day, and I could see the Olympic Mountains on the Olympic Peninsula. I knew I needed to retake the exam, but felt totally defeated. I said out loud to myself, I don't think I can do this. A couple of weeks later, when I had collected myself, I was walking from my car into the hospital and caught myself whistling the hymn, *Great is Thy Faithfulness*. I smiled to myself and thought, I guess I'll do this until I get it right.

Until the very moment of writing this, I hadn't made the connection that this is exactly what I said to myself when I stepped off the troop plane in Thailand, seeing all of the rice patties, and knowing I had a year ahead of me away from Joyce.

After a year, I lost the job at Good Samaritan. So I decided to continue my association with the Family Physician in Tacoma and expand the hours I worked there. Some friends who were in private practice urged me to be available for evening work at least until eight p.m. and maybe even Saturday mornings. This way, people who could afford counseling could see me without missing work during the week. Even the physician I was working with echoed this recommendation. However, if I did this, I would not be available to attend baseball and basketball games, water polo games, or to have dinner with everyone when they got home. So I decided I'd work no evenings or Saturdays. As it was, I wouldn't get home until six p.m.

Around this time, in 1986, an opportunity came up to begin adjunct teaching at Pacific Lutheran University, which I did for the next five years, teaching one or two courses a semester. I took the exam again. This time, I got 75 percent passing. I had been told when I started my doctoral work that if one had the intelligence to complete a traditional on-campus master's degree, they were smart enough to complete a doctorate. The difference between the two was tenacity. Yep! By the time I left the practice, after seven years, it had grown to three and a half days a week, and I was scheduled a month ahead.

Enlightenment

The ordeal between taking the exam the first time in 1984 and when I passed it in 1986 was accompanied by periods of exhilaration from realizing how well I knew the field of psychology, and on the other hand, frustration and disappointment from coming so close to passing and knowing that in most other states I had passed. There were also times of second-guessing my decision to pursue the licensed psychologist route, and self-doubt about being smart enough. There were even times when I heard the words of my high school guidance counselor in my head: that college wasn't for me, and that I should find an easy trade school. It's easy to get so focused through emotional reasoning, and losing sight of our rational side, on a failure that we lose sight of the bigger picture: I had already completed my BA, MA, and PhD; had success at major universities, Pacific Lutheran University, Oregon State University, and the University of Washington, etc., etc. Christian Parables and Buddhist koans, which, when I take them to heart, tell us about the foolishness of my self-flagellation.

During these times, our heightened emotions can cause us to lose sight of the rational and factual evidence all around us. Or the other way around, we can get too focused on only the facts that we lose touch with our emotional knowing. We're healthiest when we have a balance of both ways of reasoning. These elevated emotions can also help us see positive aspects of the situation we might otherwise not see, provided we remain empty enough of our regrets and anticipations, to seeing them. The potentially positive, and key aspect comes when we can admit that what we thought we knew, what we were sure would happen, might not happen, or maybe doesn't really matter at all.

In the Zen tradition, our personal ground zero of not knowing is where we need to start from.[2] A parable in Luke 2 tells of a rich man who is about to decide to tear down his barns and build bigger ones so he is secure, in his own strength, many times over, long into the future. But he is told by God that he is a fool and that he is about to die that night.

---

2. Lehrhaurt, Roshi Linda Myopia Ryugo, (2026) *Fierce Determination,* in Lion's Roar, pg. 40-45

Buddhism stresses the fact that we really have no hold on the future. NOW is all we have. When we can empty ourselves of the past, successes and failures, and hopes and anticipation of the future, we set the stage for enlightenment.

So I had missed passing by a half percentage point and lost the rehabilitation hospital job. After a few days, I had taken a deep breath and I concluded that there was only one thing I could do about this, retake the exam. I knew my scores were within the plus or minus standard error, so it was a matter of time. We were making ends meet with adjunct teaching at PLU, the private practice was growing, and Joyce was teaching in a public school. I retook it. It always took about six weeks to get the results. This time, I decided life would go on as usual and not expect an early notification. Even so, I dreamt about the questions on the test and finally getting the letter in the mail. A few weeks before the results were due to arrive, we decided to get away for the weekend.

A Personal Koan[3]

We went to our favorite weekend retreat. A rustic lodge on Whidbey Island that looks out on Puget Sound. I was really doing pretty well at not thinking about it. We were sitting by a fire in a large stone fireplace in the lounge, waiting for our dinner reservation. I began thumbing through a magazine and turned to an article that caught my attention in a business magazine, *The Superman Syndrome*. It was by a forty-something, self-described "golden boy": all-state high school and college football star, 4.0 student, decorated veteran fighter pilot, and CEO of a Fortune 500 company. He was the picture of self-confidence. Each of these accolades along the way had opened the door for the next opportunity. Then some catastrophe happened, and he hit bottom, big time, and he realized that all of his successes had meant nothing. His world fell apart, he had nothing. As I was reading, an epiphany hit me. Which, today I would refer to as an enlightenment. Although I had been anything but a golden boy, I

---

3. Koan: a paradoxical anecdote or riddle, used in Zen Buddhism to demonstrate the inadequacy of logical reasoning and to provoke enlightenment.

had subconsciously been focusing on what I didn't have, the stardom. I was always trying to make up for what, in my own eyes, I was not. Tears filled my eyes and began rolling down my cheeks. Joyce looked at me and asked what I was reading. She picked up the business magazine and gave me a puzzled look. I told her I was going outside for a few moments. I walked down onto a pier that was on the water and sat there and wept, with relief. Joyce followed me and asked if I was ok. Through the tears, I told her I was actually great. I told her about the article and that I realized how much I had been striving and trying to be something I wasn't. And all (four) of the exams I had failed had been the fear that "they", whoever they were, were going to find out I didn't have what it took. For the first time I felt ok with who I was, exactly as I was.

Two weeks later, I got the results of the exam and had passed it with the required 75 percent. With hindsight, I believe this enlightenment would not have happened at that time without the emotional striving and clinging to what I believed should/must happen for me in order to be at peace. I was ripe. Whew, peace like a river! Its important to know that this enlightenment is not a once and for all experience. This experience continues to bear fruit continually, daily, or at least regularly and frequently. Because of my focused study of Buddhism the reminders of being in the now, here and now, come much quicker. Meditation serves as an avenue for this for me. It is a way of centering, as William James refers to it, of keeping my spiritual self at the core of who I am.

PART 5

chapter 9

New Thread - Professor

ADDING Wesleyan/Anglian Theology

Upon leaving the charismatic church, I didn't attend any church for over a year. This was mainly due to my disenchantment with that form of Christianity. Joyce was still teaching at Peoples' Christian School, and a condition of her employment was that she attend church there. So, she attended on Sunday mornings. At the end of her contract year, she resigned from her teaching position. Matt, our youngest, started attending the Nazarene church in town with a friend in middle school. We eventually began attending with him. We were both familiar with the Wesleyan doctrine from our time at the college where we met. The attraction had to do with, as I understood it, the emphasis on an attitude, or intent, of our soul or heart toward God, versus the emphasis on emotional responses, which was characteristic of Pentecostalism, and on keeping the rules of my Baptist roots. Joyce and I stayed in the Church of the Nazarene for 24 years.

MNU

As mentioned, I continued teaching a couple of courses a semester at Pacific Lutheran University, along with a private practice with the family physician. I stayed in that practice seven years. I also taught an occasional course at a local community college and graduate counseling courses at Chapman College at McChord Air Force Base. These teaching opportunities provided some excellent experiences skills. I discovered how much I loved teaching and private practice. After attending a local Nazarene church for a few years, the pastor encouraged me to look into teaching at Nazarene University. Matt would graduate from high school in the spring of '91. So, it seemed like a good time for me to consider a change. I took the pastor's advice and sent out my resume. I accepted a psychology faculty position at a Nazarene university in Olathe, Kansas. I loved teaching in a setting where I had the freedom and was encouraged to integrate my faith with contemporary psychology. We were there at MNU for 19 years. I loved teaching and the relationships I developed with students. I tried to encourage them to think outside of their roots.

Some excellent work by James Fowler proposes a stage-wise development of faith that parallels Erik Erikson's social-emotional stages of psychological development.[1] *Typical first-year college students identify strongly with the values of others who have influenced them, such as their parents. They often accept matters of faith uncritically, without serious questioning, which is in line with their parents and other influential adults. Students who attend conservative religious colleges similar to their faith of origin, unless challenged, hold on to their parents' faith. Students who get through college and continue into early adulthood with this foreclosed faith, or, for that matter, foreclosed political, vocational, and social views as well, are more apt to postpone critical questioning and to own their own reasoning until later in adulthood. The impact of this is that they are more likely to face crisis-like questioning later in adult life. Think mid-life crisis. This is one reason many colleges encourage semester, or longer, experiences abroad. Experiencing cultures that differ from their*

---

1. Fowler, James (1976) *Stages of Faith,* Harper Collins Publisher

" " (200) *Becoming Adult Becoming Christian,* Jossey-Bass Publisher

own are more likely to develop their own sense of values. Research tells us that over seventy percent of us, by the time we are in our thirties, settle into values similar to the ones with which we were raised. Although those values may not be exactly the same, they are in the same ballpark. So, instead of being in the same political party, at least the importance of politics is similar.

Before we actually moved to Kansas from Washington, I began applying for my psychology license in Kansas. A colleague in Washington, who was originally from the Midwest, said I might have trouble getting licensed in Kansas. The reputation of the Kansas Board of Professional Psychology (Behavioral Sciences Regulatory Board, [BSRB]) was a closed shop. They limited the number of people to whom they granted licenses in order to limit the competition. The BSRB did this through a quirky (my word) regulation for people coming into the state who were already licensed in other states. The passing score on the national exam was the same as in Washington. I was good there. All other states that required post-doctoral supervision required one year of post-doc supervision *before* applying for licensing. A few states did not even require that. Kansas, on the other hand, was the only state that required two years of post-doctoral supervision work before getting licensed. This supervised work had to be done before getting licensed. This meant that if you already had a psychology license, you couldn't get *pre-licensed* supervised experience because you already had your license. Thus, the number of people coming in from other states was limited. However, because I had had trouble passing the exam in Washington, I did have two years of supervision prior to getting licensed. So, I was good here also, or so I thought.

They denied my license because Washington (wait for it) did not *require* the two years.

So, I appealed and testified before the board. They still denied it. I was disappointed and frustrated. Topeka, Kansas, the state capital, is where the board met. Topeka was about an hour from our house in Olathe. When I got home, Joyce told me there was a message on our phone for me. It was from the Assistant Attorney General who sat on the licensing board that I needed to call her. When she answered the phone, she told me the conversation was off the record and that she would deny having spoken to me. She said that I needed to hire an attorney. I told her I was new to Kansas and didn't have any contacts. She said she would also deny this part of the conversation as well and gave me the name of an attorney who had fought with the licensing board in prior years. I contacted him, and he could guide me through the process of confronting the BSRB.

By the time the drama was finished, I had hired the lawyer, testified before a Kansas State House Committee, and gone to court before a judge. I knew I was right. So, three years after my initial application, I got a letter from the Assistant State Attorney General saying that the board, under pressure, was changing the regulation to require only one year, in line with all other states. This would allow for a kinder reciprocity for psychologists desiring to move to Kansas. And here is the cherry on top. They were calling the amendment the *Henning Amendment*. I have the letter framed on my office wall at home. Tenacity.

I still had to pass an oral exam governing the practice of psychology. The thirty-minute interview before the BSRB went as smooth as glass, and they said they would grant me the license. As I walked out of the interview, a board member followed me out and stopped me. She wanted to congratulate me. She had been on the board at my first meeting three years prior, and she was delighted I had persevered.

Before I drove out of Topeka, I found a florist and ordered a dozen red roses delivered to the attorney who had told me to get an attorney. The note on it read: *"Thank You for Your Support." And of course, this is off the record, and I would deny having done this.*

I don't know if this is a side note or a central point. At any rate, if I had not hung in there and taken the exam until I finally got the 75, Kansas would not have recognized my score as passing by its standard. Which would have meant I would not have had a Kansas Psychology License and therefore could not have worked for the Rehab Institute of Kansas City. All things work together.

During the first semester at MNU I was shown how to do academic advising, complete the necessary paperwork, and recommend courses for the first couple of semesters. I inadvertently registered a male student into a women's P.E. class. He didn't mind that at all, but the instructor told him that this wasn't going to fly.

One other male freshman walked into my office. With hindsight, he probably looked a lot like I had at that age. Round-faced and plump. As we began, he immediately told me he had some things we needed to work around for his class schedule. First, he was turning out for football. (He didn't look the college football type.) So even though practice didn't really start until 4:00 p.m., he couldn't have any classes that ended after 3:00 p.m. in order to have time to get to practice. Second, he needed to sleep in the morning to get enough rest, so there would be no classes before 9:00 a.m., preferably not before 10:00; third, there would be no classes at 12:00 because he needed to eat lunch with his friends. So that translated into two morning and two afternoon slots for his classes. I immediately thought of my first two semesters in college. Karma?

Although there are no perfect jobs, getting to teach full-time was a dream come true. I'll talk a little later about some frustrations, but I loved this opportunity and would not have traded this time in my life. At MNU, teaching has always been the priority. Professors were not required to do research or to publish. In my mind, this had both positive and negative aspects to it. I decided to take advantage of being in an academic institution and strove to write and present papers at scholarly conferences over the nineteen years I was there. I presented at conferences in the U.S. and Canada. It was a highlight to also present at international conferences: twice at the summer C.S. Lewis conferences in Oxford, England, and at a European conference on Psyche and Faith in the Netherlands. Most of the papers I wrote during my time in Kansas were about the integration of Christian faith and contemporary psychology.

Professionally, once I got my license to practice psychology straightened out, I started looking around for an opportunity to do some part-time clinical work at a rehabilitation facility. Because of my bachelor's degree and experience in physical rehabilitation, I've always had an affinity for rehabilitation psychology. The Neuropsychologist at The Rehabilitation Institute of Kansas City (TRIKC) was interested in having me do some work for them as a Rehabilitation Psychology Fellow. After completing the fellowship, I continued working part-time for them. I was with them for ten years. My time at TRIKC was very fulfilling and a highlight of my clinical career. I've often thought that if I had discovered neuropsychology when I was making career decisions back in the VA days, I would have gone that route. I enjoyed two facets of Neuro and Rehab Psychology. First was the assessment process of sorting through a complex puzzle-like situation of impaired behavior and cognitive skills. Upon solving this puzzle, we would help guide a plan to improve the individual's functioning and increase their quality of life to the highest level possible. Second, and equally fulfilling, was the privilege of working with patients who often felt like they'd fallen headfirst, into a pit of despair. Then, I had the privilege of helping them climb back out of the hole. Part of this process involved cognitive assessments to pinpoint the cognitive deficits and the best way to rehab. I also enjoyed the team approach to rehabilitation and the collaboration with physical therapists, occupational therapists, nursing personnel, speech and language therapists, physicians, and the patient's family. It was a very fulfilling work!

chapter 10

Multi-Cultural Threads

EUROPE

When it came time for my sabbatical at MNU, I was fortunate to get a position at European Nazarene College (EuNC) in Switzerland. I taught psychology courses and acted as a campus counselor. Joyce took a month's leave of absence from Special Education and joined me. We both were smitten with the experience of living with students and faculty from Western and Eastern Europe, as well as Asia. EuNC was located on the picturesque Rhine River. When we returned from Switzerland in December 2000, we began conversations about the possibility of semi-permanent positions at EuNC.

A year after our return home, during Thanksgiving, 2001, we took advantage of an invitation to travel to Moscow, Russia. This was just two months following the attack on the U.S. on 9/11/2001. Even though things were pretty stressful in the airports, especially for international flights, we didn't feel like we could pass up this opportunity. The reason for going was the rare opportunity to teach a class on marriage and family to Missionaries from all over Eastern Europe, Russia, and Asia. The intent was that the missionaries could then teach about healthy marriage and family to the native peoples in their regions. This turned out to be a true highlight of our lives.

A few days before returning home, a Moscow missionary, Davide Cantarella, was giving us a walking tour of the city. It was Sunday, and we had just each purchased a hamburger and fries at the then-largest McDonald's restaurant in the world. We took the burgers to-go and were walking through an open market when a couple of adolescent boys approached us. The boys asked if they could have Davide's half-eaten hamburger and fries. Which, of course, Davide immediately gave to them. What impressed me was that they weren't asking for money. They were hungry. Later in the day, we rode subway to our hotel to get our luggage. It was really crowded—standing room only. As we were getting off at our stop, Davide subtly slipped a man, standing with his family, a handful of rubles (Russian currency). In later discussions about these two instances, Davide explained, as we had heard earlier in the week from Russian citizens themselves, that since Communism fell, people were actually poorer than when it was in place. Capitalism wasn't working so well, ten years following the fall, for the huddled masses. Similar to the working poor in the U.S. that fall between the cracks and can't afford health care, can't support a family on minimum wage or get kicked off the welfare rolls.

Something we don't seem to understand in the U.S. is that after decades, eighty years in Russia's case, of Communist rule, capitalism isn't like a pill that is taken and things get better in a couple of months. Missionaries explained that a McDonaldization, fast food approach, doesn't work for the gospel either. It usually takes at least three generations for significant cultural and societal change. So, just as we have found in past decades, supporting regime change in authoritarian countries and enforcing a system that "appears" to be a democratic system often doesn't last.

Because of our very positive experiences in Switzerland during my sabbatical, we began talking about applying for semi-permanent teaching positions at EuNC. EuNC is part of the Church of the Nazarene system of higher education. As part of preparing for a teaching position at EuNC, I knew I needed to complete some graduate-level seminary work focused on Wesleyan theology. So, to meet that Cross-Cultural Ministries at the Nazarene Theological Seminary in Kansas City. MNU was gracious in allowing me to adjust my teaching schedule to my seminary coursework. I did this while also continuing to work part-time at The Rehabilitation Institute.

In June 2002, Joyce and I each accepted a two-year position at EuNC. Joyce would teach English as a Second Language (ESL), and I would teach psychology and spiritual formation courses and serve as the campus counselor. Scott was married and in the Army, paying back his obligation for attending medical school. He was in Germany. Matt was living in Texas and working as a traveling nurse. So we reasoned this would be a good time for an adventure. We felt this was an opportunity of a lifetime. The cross-cultural experience was truly enriching.

A significant insight for us was the extent to which culture shapes religious doctrine and practice. Some behaviors and beliefs considered evidence of spiritual maturity in one culture were not seen that way in others. One example was the drinking alcohol. The majority of students from Europe had grown up in families and environments that drank alcohol. It was a way of life. The Church of the Nazarene (CotN) has a manual that guides the behavioral practices of its members. It prohibits the consumption of alcohol. (The Manual is written in the U.S.; the general headquarters for the CotN is in Kansas.) More than one student confided that even though they said they didn't, they actually drank in private or when they were home or just turned a blind eye when they saw it being drunk by fellow students, friends, and family.

Another example of cultural influence came from a student living in a country in Africa. He explained that in that culture, everything an individual owns is considered communal—belonging to the entire village. So when you asked for money from one person to help you out, you were under no actual obligation to pay it back. Failing to pay it back was not a crime, a sin, or even considered selfish. In more communal societies, helping each other is part of the basic value system. This sounds similar to what we know about the lifestyles of Jesus, Buddha, and their followers. Traveling as itinerant teachers, with only the clothes they carried and eating with the people they met.

For the students at EuNC who came from these more communal, or collectivist, societies, naturally brought these cooperative values with them. When it came to studying, this communal living and support was quite acceptable and even encouraged This mutual assistance for writing papers was also acceptable, as long as the finished product was that of the individual student's effort. However, when taking exams, we wanted to know what the individual student had learned. Cooperating to graduate by bringing cheat sheets into the exam and looking at a neighbor's paper was viewed by faculty members from the U.S. and Western Europe, as cheating. Students from traditionally Eastern cultures often saw this as a form of cooperation for learning and shared goals.

There is an excellent novel by Barbara Kingsolver, The Poisonwood Bible.[1] *Kingsolver describes the struggles, insights, and failures of a white missionary family from a southern U. S. state who go on their own to the Congo to convert the naked natives. I was reading this while on sabbatical at EuNC. This is a book that, when finished, I immediately began reading it a second time.*

One U.S. student who attended EuNC for a semester, was shocked when the dining hall had pumpkins and other seasonal decorations on the tables. Because pumpkins were associated with Halloween in the U.S., she tried to convince everyone that this was akin to devil worship. She struggled with cultural issues her entire semester she was there.

Realizing that these differences are forms of cultural relativism often contributes to the growth and broadening of one's worldview, which is necessary in mature adulthood. Some naive U. S students voiced difficulty accepting that C.S. Lewis would meet with his friends, the Inklings, at a pub to discuss their writing over a pint of beer, or that he smoked cigarettes.

The Unexpected

Our initial commitment to EuNC was for two years, with the option to extend if things were going well. However, one factor I had not anticipated was my progressive hearing loss. By this time, in the progression, I was wearing hearing aids in both ears. Because the loss was gradual, I had, without being altogether aware of it, learned how to read facial

---

1. Kingsolver, Barbara (1998) *The Poisnwood Bible,* Harper Publisher, A Pulitzer Prize Finalist

expressions to better understand speech. My actual hearing was steadily getting worse. At regular intervals, I went to an audiologist to have my hearing aids adjusted—about every eighteen months. Each time I would go to an appointment, it was like I was experiencing the loss anew. But I would be thankful that the technology was progressing as well I could continue teaching, and doing clinical work. The inverse of watching a child grow, who does so in spurts and starts, and is never smooth, my hearing loss was becoming worse in starts and spurts also. So even though I had just been to EuNC 18 months prior, I had become significantly harder of hearing, which I had not anticipated.

With hindsight, I've realized that an essential part of reading lips and facial expressions is pairing what I interpret the facial expressions to mean, with the way words sound that I'm used to hearing. Most of the students, even though they were fluent in English, spoke with accents from their native countries. Thus, I was really struggling with new pronunciations that differed from what I was used to. Plus, without realizing it, this ability to have my hearing aids adjusted was actually facilitating my denial that I really was steadily and rather rapidly going deaf. After all, I saw other older men with hearing aids that looked just like mine, and they seemed fine. I hadn't put two and two together that the steady, fairly rapid decline would, sooner rather than later, end up in total deafness.

I had learned to rely on reading lips and facial expressions, which worked well in the U.S., where I could also rely on tone of voice and enunciation. But teaching in a setting where all of my students and many colleagues were second-language English speakers turned out to be an altogether different story. I was constantly having to have students repeat questions and, in other instances, ask another student what someone else had said. This was quite stressful. So, a little over halfway through our first year, we realized this wasn't working. With much thought, regret, and prayer, we asked to be released from our two-year commitment and return to the States at the end of the first year. What a disappointment! EuNC was understanding, but certainly not happy with me. By losing a psychology professor, campus counselor, and ESL teacher, they were being left in the lurch.

Fortunately, a former student with experience living in Europe and a master's degree in counseling took my place. Michelle turned out to be a great fit. She stayed at EuNC for several years.

MNU had not filled their position I vacated a year earlier, so I could step back into my role there as assistant academic dean and psychology professor. I also went back to work part-time at the Rehab Institute. Although Joyce's position as Special Ed District Facilitator had been filled, she could step back into her Special Ed position at her old school. My audiologist told me that my hearing had continued to deteriorate and that I should progress to the next level of care. This would eventually probably lead to a cochlear implant. In the interim, I started using a receiver that hung around my neck and communicated directly into my upgraded hearing aids. So, I was back in business. This was the spring of 2003. I would stay at MNU until the spring of 2010.

Acquired hearing loss, like mine, differs from being born deaf in that I continued to live in a hearing world. Joyce and I tried, on at least three different occasions, to learn American Sign Language. However, those classes were for hearing individuals who wanted to learn sign language to work in the field. As such, the instructors were also hearing and would move faster than we could follow. Plus, because we lived in a hearing world, we used sign language only in class. So we never really got the hang of it. Had we been younger, we may have been able to pick it up more easily.

LGBTQA+

An important cultural issue at present for the Church of The Nazarene is whether or not there will be acceptance and affirmation of LGBTQA+ individuals. Many conservative Christian organizations, rather than actually struggling with what to do as the culture has shifted beneath their feet on this issue, are approaching it as black and white, sin or no sin. There appears to be no middle ground. Although this is not divided by cultural location, as the drinking of alcohol was/is in Europe, the sharp divisions run along more conservative and liberal lines, as well as by age. This was an issue at the recent gathering of the General Assembly of the CotN in 2023. Individuals who are affirming or accepting of LGBTQA+ people as members and leaders in the church are being told they need to surrender their papers of ordination if they are in a position of leadership, or it's suggested they would be happier worshiping elsewhere. Even though we left the CotN in 2008, eighteen years ago, this lack of acceptance of gays was a primary and motivating factor for our exit. Plus, we had been feeling an increasing attraction to the Episcopal Church for several years. Part of this attraction was that I knew queer individuals who attended Episcopal congregations and felt accepted.

The black-and-white, love-it-or-leave-it, right-or-wrong rarely does either side any good over the long term. Attempting to force individuals into changing doesn't result in lasting change but only serves to rob the square peg, , of its distinctive edges that make for a unique individual. This goes on until they're finally forced out. If an individual temporarily puts up with being made to look like everyone else, at least on the outside, as a matter of survival, they are building up walls on the inside.

Thinking specifically about LGBTQA+ youth: recent research on suicide among youth has concluded that the reason we haven't made a dent in the rate of suicide deaths is that the focus of prevention has most often been on individualized solutions, rather than systemic, interconnected solutions. Systemic solutions need to address protective factors, such as faith communities and family ties. Interestingly, social and political contexts have a significant impact on youth in general and LGBTQA+ youth specifically. Higher rates of suicide attempts are found in youth who report that their homes, schools, and communities [think communities of faith] are not accepting. To make this point, in states that proposed anti-LBGTQA+ legislation, texts to the Crisis Text Line rose by a statistically significant amount in the subsequent four weeks. We essentially have youth existing in an environment that is pervasively invalidating. Pervasive feelings of sadness or hopelessness among LGBTQA+ students is 69%. This is compared with the general population, where 57% of girls and 29% of boys are affected.[2]

Without the affirmation, and often with outright condemnation, of who these young people are, they are being forced to seek outside affirmation, if they

---

2. Monitor on Psychology (a publication of the American Psychological Association), July/August, 2023, pg 54-61 *seek it at all. If they are prone to be religious, they often see their only option as going outside their faith of origin. Because of the vulnerability that youth face during this time of development, this lack of validation only increases the likelihood of depression, isolation, and suicidal ideation.*

This means there's a tremendous need for more systemic solutions to youth suicide and even higher rates of suicide among LGBTQA+ youth. Significant and purposeful efforts to change the systems of faith in which our youth find themselves are essential. Or, if their faith of origin communities won't change, we must help guide these young people to find a community in which they feel accepted and validated. To do anything less is self-centered—loving an organization more than the individuals within it.

chapter 11

More Threads –
SEE SOMETHING, SAY SOMETHING

The title of this chapter borrows from the signs seen at airports urging everyone to be alert to potential dangers, such as bombs left in unattended bags. The assumption is that we all have a responsibility to be alert. This can and should be applied to social injustice we see, and to do something about it. Even though I really enjoyed my time teaching at a Christian university, the most frustrating element was the absence of faculty members of color, which is directly related to a lack of students of color. Athletics, football and track, were often the primary point of entry to college for students of color. However, without faculty members of color, the possibility of these students finding a faculty member with whom they could identify is limited. The result a relatively small number actually graduated. This situation is true nationally across private colleges and universities. Catholic universities have a higher percentage of these students. Public institutions have a somewhat better percentage than private institutions. Although still below the national average of people of color as compared to the general population, public institutions are more likely to have student and faculty populations that begin to approach the national percentage.

Institutional and Systemic Racism Inside Christian Higher Education

I have read and re-read, written and rewritten this section several times. I hope the reader will read this section with the same level of concern, dare I say love, with which I have written it. It is probably obvious how passionate I am about this subject. I don't intend to shame or cause offense. I am speaking now of what I saw during twenty-five years at university teaching, from 1986 to 2010, as well as being a student over a period of 20 years. For me, not saying something about what I saw in plain sight would make me complicit. It's always better to say something about a package that could be a bomb and have it turn out to be nothing than to assume it is nothing and have it turn out to be an explosive. I feel the same about racism—to see something that is racist and not say something makes us all complicit. I realize that, as a white man, there are instances of racism, systemic or individual, which I overlook. The pastor of the African American church that we attended for several years told me once that I notice things that a lot of white people don't see. I wish that more white people would get keyed in to the racist ways in the U.S.

Except for one Black faculty member whom I helped pave the way to get hired, I don't remember any Black faculty members. When I arrived at the last college where I taught, there were no Black faculty, adjunct or full-time, nor when I left nineteen years later. The explanation given when I brought this up was that no qualified black individuals ever applied for the positions. This is a perfect example of institutional/systemic racism. This is much more than a simple, straightforward problem with a simple solution. Just waiting for a qualified black person to apply is like waiting to be offered a job I'm qualified for without actively seeking it by visiting websites, filling out application forms, and so forth. The way has to be paved and repaved, year after year. Part of paving the way may involve encouraging junior and senior high school students to consider careers in teaching and research at the university level. Then, as they approach considering a career in academics, it is essential to stay in touch and continue encouraging them by helping them search for scholarships and find a college that will welcome them for their intellectual potential. Many students of color are first-generation students. This means they won't know how to navigate both academic and social life in a university environment. Second- and third-generation students have heard their parents, relatives, and friends talk about college life beyond just studying. This is all college preparation. I have just barely scratched the surface of how purposeful and committed the long-range solutions must be.

To illustrate how entrenched the problem of institutional bias is in my own academic experiences. I began attending college in 1964 and completed my doctoral program in 1983. I continued to complete residencies and fellowships through 2008. This spans over fifty years. This includes both private, conservative Christian colleges and more liberal Christian colleges, as well as state public institutions. I can't remember a single black faculty member that I had during those fifty years.

Even though individual faculty and administrators may not be personally racist, the system in which they work behaves in a racist fashion. I start here with the assumption that none of, or at least very few of, the faculty and administrators were/are personally racist. It is up to each individual to search their own soul about this. However, what I do believe is that some individuals behave and think in racist ways because of their cultural background.

Bias and prejudice are learned from a very early age and become a default way of thinking. As humans, we develop the ability to pre-judge experiences based on early teaching and experiences. This is part of our evolutionary survival-of-the-fittest nature. This way, we don't have to relearn something every time we face the same or similar situations. Prejudice is, simply put, judging before you know the facts When driving, we pre-judge which intersections are likely to be more treacherous, so we approach them cautiously. We try to teach our young children to be prejudiced against strangers who try to lure them into their cars. This is a protective function of prejudice.

Thirty years ago, we were at an upscale shopping area in Kansas City. Joyce and I had gone there for dinner and were looking through some of the shops. It was a lovely evening, lots of people were walking on the sidewalks, and many had shopping bags. We were standing at a crosswalk waiting for the WALK sign. Several people were waiting beside us. Three black teenage boys walked up, joking and laughing as teenagers do. The car in front of us, waiting for the light to change, suddenly locked its doors. The click was loud. The boys laughed and said in a loud voice, "don't worry, my daddy's car is worth much more than yours is." The driver had not seen the need to lock the doors before, but suddenly did so when they saw the black boys. This is racist. I'm not suggesting we shouldn't be careful. If this situation had occurred only for the sake of safety, the doors would already have been locked. I realize I don't know what was going on exactly in the driver's mind. But I'd bet the driver's behavior was nothing more than a reflexive act of prejudice. On its own, this may be a relatively minor thing. But when it is part of a pattern, it is suggestive of an attitude of prejudice and racism.

Unless we deliberately set out to change the harmful, learned and reflexive prejudices and biases we hold, they will remain automatic and unchecked. A senior administrator at a Christian university I taught at for several years once told me, in response to his prejudiced comments in a conversation we were having, that, after all, he had been raised in Texas. This highly educated, otherwise kind, and Christian individual seemed to think this excused his prejudices. These origins of racial discrimination reach back to the 1500s in Europe, and as such are part of our cultural DNA. Capitalism at that time functioned in purposefully racist and prejudiced ways to justify colonialism, including the slave trade industry.[1]

During my early years in the Midwest, I tried to understand how systemic racism exists in Christian organizations. *The* lack-of-faculty-of-color is pervasive across conservative religious organizations, which tend to be relatively closed systems. Open employment positions are rarely advertised outside of the existing social network of smaller conservative Christian universities and colleges. A national search, for example, would include, but not be limited to, posting jobs in the *Chronicle of Higher Education.*[2] This lack of national searches is due in part to institutions' unwillingness to accept individuals from other faiths, and the uncomfortable situation of having to reject them when they are actually academically qualified. At least, that was the case when I was involved in private universities 16 years ago. The most common method of finding

---

1. Jennings, Willie James (2010) *The Christian Imagination: Theology and the Origins of Race,* Yale University Press

2. *The Chronicle of Higher Education* is a publication which has job postings around the country. 38,000 jobs were listed in recent editions.

applicants was word of mouth and listing openings on their own websites. Therefore, the typical white faculty member is unlikely to have connections with black academics seeking a university job. This is an example of how institutional and systemic bias and racism operate. When a system is entrenched in this way, purposeful steps are the only way change happens.

During my first year at my last university, the Rodney King trial and Los Angeles riots of the early nineties had just taken place.[3] I worked this critical social and cultural issue into class lectures and discussions. I quizzed students on how their other professors had brought this up. The answer was that none had. I was grieved by what happened in LA and that no other professors, at least for the students with whom I had contact, had seen the need to address this in a college class. Was this because white professors aren't as keyed into the plights of Black people? I heard a Jessie Jackson speech on television about the trial and riots. (I've always liked to listen to people like Rev. Jackson because he usually provokes me to think more critically.) He emphasized the importance of supporting programs that address systemic racism at both national and local levels. He also stressed the importance of improving educational opportunities. Education is one way to combat systemic prejudices. As a result, Joyce and I considered supporting the United Negro College Fund, but thought that would have little impact on attracting or keeping African American Students to where I was teaching.

We had sold our house in Washington when we moved to the midwest. We were renting at the time and getting ready to buy a house. It seemed important to use a portion of our profit as a tithe to support students of color at MNU. I asked how much would be needed to establish an endowed scholarship. Although it was a little more than the tithe of our profit, we decided this was what we should do. We endowed a scholarship specifically for African American students majoring in Education or Psychology. I also had regular deductions taken from my paycheck, into the endowment over the 19 years we were there. We reasoned that Education and Psychology were two majors with the potential to prepare

---

3. It is interesting that the name of the *victims* is often used in identifying trials such as these, rather than the name of the perpetrators: *Rodney King, George Floyd, Michael Brown, Breanna Tyler, etc., etc.*

students to become leaders in these professions. Which in turn has the greatest chance of encouraging college students of color, as well as those younger students of color in public schools to consider going to college. That scholarship has undergone some changes in name in recent years, but remains in place. We get a thank-you note from the recipient each spring.

Martin Luther King, Jr

An experience that reinforced the direction I was thinking and moving, and that I needed to push harder for change, happened during a Spring Break in the early 1990s. We took a road trip from Olathe, Kansas, to New Orleans through Missouri, Tennessee, and Alabama. We stopped in Birmingham, Alabama, at the church where Martin Luther King Jr. had preached. The basement was a recently opened museum. The museum's walls had Murals depicting the civil rights movement of the mid-twentieth century. We walked around the room and looked at the pictures of black people being knocked down with spray from fire hoses, attacked by police dogs, and the marches of that era. I was struck that the only depiction of white people was of the police, Governor George Wallis, and Ku Klux Klan members. This is how whites were, and often still are, viewed by blacks. It also brought home that this was all going on in Alabama, only a short drive to Mississippi, while we were stationed in the Air Force in Biloxi in 1967-68.

As we left the museum and got back on the road, I was overwhelmed emotionally by how unaware I had been of the plight and oppression of Black People during that time and into the present. Racism and oppression always seem to have their own incongruity with Christianity as practiced in the U.S., not just in the South. A memory that completely slipped my mind until recently is of the billboard greeting sign as you entered Alabama on the freeway in the late 1960s. I forget the exact number, but the sign read, '68,000 Alabama Baptists Welcome You.' There, in the land of Baptists, was socially and legally entrenched racism. This kind of oversight by me was, and is, an example of how overt racism sustains itself. This is an example of why racial inequality and its roots must be taught in schools rather than continuously trying to bury them. If we are going to learn from our history, we must be made uncomfortable. We have to learn from the past and not repeat it. Because I was already becoming *woke*[4] by my young and mid-adult years, I believe I had the ability to learn about the social injustices of that time—if only I had been taught.

OLATHE, KANSAS

Besides the scholarship we had established, we believed we should also be financially and physically supporting institutions that enrich African Americans' lives in the local area. It's one thing for white people of the majority to send money to impoverished areas. It is quite another thing to actually join with them. Twenty-five miles from our house was an African American Nazarene Church, Blue Hills, in the heart of inner-city Kansas City, Missouri. We attended a few times, then spoke with the pastor. We said we enjoyed attending and wanted to know, since we were the only white people in the early service, whether we'd be welcome as members. His response was a very gracious, "Of course." African American neighborhood churches are much more likely to be a center of social life in their local communities than urban white churches. This seems especially true of megachurches, which draw from all over a large metropolitan area.

We joined the Blue Hills Church of the Nazarene and attended there for eight years until moving to Switzerland. As members, this was where our tithe and other contributions went. This was a spiritually and culturally rich experience for us. As members, we were more aware of the ongoing struggles and successes of the church. It also provided the opportunity to be aware of and support the clothing and food bank by haunting garage sales for clothes and buying food in bulk. There were occasionally other white people who attended, mostly from the local Nazarene Seminary in the same general area of Kansas City. All the church parking was on the surrounding streets. It was not uncommon to find bullet shell casings in the areas where we parked. Neither was it uncommon to have

---

4. Woke: To be woke is a compliment. I strive to be increasingly aware of social injustice against all marginalized peoples, Then strive to do something about those injustices that non-white, LGBTQA+, poor, homeless people experience day-in-and-day-out.

an announcement in the church bulletin of a funeral for a young person killed by violence whose mother attended the church. As white people in the United States, we have no idea what it is like to live under this strategically structured oppression, which reaches back at least six hundred years.

The organist at Blue Hills was an elementary school principal whose school was in the heart of the inner city. His school was old and dilapidated, consisting of two buildings separated by a playground. The main building had hot and cold running water in the bathrooms. The smaller building, which housed upper grades, had only cold water in the bathrooms. This was in the mid-1990s in Kansas City, Kansas. This man had graduated from my university MNU, with a degree in Education. He also had a master's degree in administration and was completing his doctorate in education. As I got to know him, I invited him to speak in one of my classes. He would also occasionally bring the church choir to sing in chapel services at MNU.

Being an alumnus of, he was aware of the lack of color among faculty, as well as the direct and indirect racism he experienced while he was a student. He was a freshman in the late 1970s. He confided in me that an administrator met with him and eleven other black male student-athletes to inform them that interracial dating was not allowed—that they could not date white girls on campus. The black student-athletes were segregated together in one dorm without air-conditioning. One day, when they returned to their rooms after football practice, someone had spray-painted on their door in big letters, "N . . . s go home, KKK." Once they found out who had done this, they reported it to the administration. The perpetrator apologized, saying he was just playing around. He was not disciplined. The incident was dropped.

The more my friend and I talked, the more he agreed to team-teach a course with me as an adjunct professor in the Sociology and Psychology departments on *Understanding Multi-Cultural Behavior.* We developed the course curriculum together, and the class was quite a success, particularly with many black athletes taking it. We even had a faculty member take the class. I really enjoyed teaching with my friend.

Later, when an opening in the Education Department arose, I encouraged him to apply. I lobbied the academic vice president and president on his behalf. The head of the Education department and some faculty members knew this man from his student days. They were very hopeful he would be hired, which he eventually was. However, after five or six years, he resigned to take another principal position in a public school. The impact of overt and covert racism gets to be too much to bear when there are other opportunities to do good.

Covert racism, or as an older African American colleague in the VA called it——under the table racism——might be challenging to identify on the surface of things by white people who want to believe that racism doesn't exist in their world. However, it does exist, then and now, and is clearly felt. A few white faculty members, because I was vocal in my support of faculty and students of color, said that I and people like me, including the President, were suffering from white guilt.

An office manager in Tacoma in the 1980s called me a bleeding heart. This was in response to my decision not to charge a poor white patient more than a token amount. This patient would bring paper bags with her tip money from her job as a waitress to pay for my services. She could not afford health insurance.

When I was Associate Academic Dean, a longtime faculty member, after much coaxing, agreed to meet with a black student's father who wanted to meet with him and me. The student was an athlete. The issue for the student was that the faculty member had made insensitive comments, singling the student out in front of his peers. He and his friends had been laughing too loudly, in the professor's opinion, as students were filing in before the beginning of the chapel service. The parent told me he wanted to know how best to deal with this and help his son. The dad was clearly glad his son was in college. During the meeting, the faculty member didn't say much, neither was he apologetic nor empathetic to what the dad was saying or asking about. Then, after the meeting, the faculty member told me the kid had a chip on his shoulder and that he (the professor) would say the same things again, should a similar situation arise. These attitudes and shunning are glaring, especially when they occur among faculty.

Another example of the spoken and felt racist attitudes that ran barely below the surface stands out in my memory. Required chapel services were held twice a week. One chapel speaker, who was a Black Caribbean American and was well-known in CotN circles, spoke on racism and prejudice. In the course of his presentation, he made a passing comparison between the evils of America's history of slavery and the evils of the Holocaust of the mid-twentieth century in Europe. If I remember correctly, he suggested that, as evil as the Holocaust was, slavery was similar and just as evil.

The world intervened and stopped Hitler after it had been going on for eleven years, 1933-1945, which went on far too long as it was. Yet slavery lasted in the U.S. for two and a half centuries from August 1619 to July 1860. Of course, the Civil War over slavery lasted a few years more. Reconstruction was thwarted only after 10 years. However, actual freedom in terms of the Civil Rights Movement did not really occur for another 100 years, until the mid-1950s and 1960s.

In response to the chapel speaker, a fellow faculty member told me one-on-one that he was *deeply offended at this comparison in a chapel service because the holocaust was so much worse,* and that these two events were obviously apples and oranges. He went on to explain that slavery ended a long time ago.

Besides the ridiculousness and Junior Highish-ness of bragging that one's favorite atrocity is worse than another atrocity (mine is bigger than yours), this was an attempt to diminish the horribleness of slavery and its ongoing legacy of oppression. I felt this was also an attempt to put me in my place. Sadly, this cultural denial is evident throughout our country today and is still accepted by millions, especially within conservative white Christianity. ,Genuine equality between the different races and the white ancestors of Europeans in the United States, is still a long way off. In 2024, Nikki Haley, a Republican candidate for president, said that the U.S. has never been a racist country, or at least that was not the intent of the nation. Yet she ignored the fact that her home state, of which she had been governor, actually seceded from the nation over slavery.

I'll mention one more incident of systemic racism, which, at first glance, may appear to be innocent on the surface, but in reality, is much more subtle. My friend told of situations when he was a student and continued when he was a professor. Many African-American males who were recruited to play football were admitted to college with very low high school GPA's, very low ACT scores. and other predictors, which indicated that, without extra academic support, they would not succeed in college. Yet this was not addressed upon acceptance and admission to college. Neither were they provided the support that would have increased their likelihood of success. The result? Many, if not most, brown-skinned male athletes would attend a couple of years or until their football eligibility expired because of low grades. It was not uncommon for these students to take a smattering of easier courses keep their eligibility to play sports. They would then leave school with no degree and sometimes as much as $80-100K of debt. When this was brought to the attention of the university administrators, the response was that these students volunteered to play football.

This may appear, at first glance, to be rather innocent, and maybe trying to level the playing field in favor of under-prepared students of color. First, there is no such thing as a level playing field when the same standards apply for success, yet without equal skill sets. At smaller colleges and universities, like many private colleges, MNU included, the athletic programs, by virtue of their memberships in athletic associations like the NAIA, are prohibited from awarding full-ride athletic scholarships. Further, the athlete's academic performance history does not meet the criteria for academic scholarships. So, these underprepared students, because they have to pay tuition through loans must pay to play. When giving young players, black or white, the opportunity to play college athletics, knowing what that may mean to their sense of pride and self-esteem at 18 and 19 years old, they are likely to accept it without considering the longer-term consequences. Then, a few short years later, they have mountains of debt with nothing to show for it. A scenario like this may be viewed as a savvy way to assemble winning athlete programs. Yet this type of seduction is a type of usury. When this disproportionately affects students of color, it is another example of systemic racism.

I'm not suggesting that all student-athletes of color fail to complete their degrees or perform well. Some do well, even very well. It would take away from those individuals' accomplishments to imply such. My friend is an example of someone who is doing well as an assistant superintendent of schools. A Black student with whom I was close, upon graduation, went on to get his MBA and is presently a minister in San Diego, California. Jermaine was a student-athlete and a NAIA All-American football and track athlete. There was an article in the Kansas City Star a couple of years ago of Major Johnny Roland of the Olathe Police Department. Major Roland was honored as the recipient of the MidAmerica Nazarene University's MLK Jr. Living Legacy Award for 2024[5]. Major Roland was also a student-athlete at MNU and had recently graduated from the FBI National Academy. The list, of course, goes on.

Given the slow rate of progress toward equality, we must remain diligent to ensure equal treatment to people of color within our Christian organizations. We need to step up and quicken the pace of progress toward *The Dream* that Martin Luther King, Jr. had: that all are created equal and that we do not judge others based on the color of a person's skin.

Students of color who have not done well and have been victims of individual and systemic racism should remind us how easy it is to take our eye off the goal, and to remind us that equal opportunities are guaranteed for all, regardless of skin color, ethnicity, gender, sexual orientation, and creed.

We are all works in progress, which is why I haven't given any identifying specifics on the outside chance that people associated with my previous university may someday read this. But this college is the example I know best as a faculty member and administrator. I have fond memories of my nearly twenty years there. I loved teaching and the relationships with students, as well as the relationships with faculty members that Joyce and I developed over that time. But I list these examples to illustrate how little we've actually accomplished in the last couple of hundred years, especially within Christian organizations. The author of the now-famous Blue-eyes Brown-eyes exercise, Jane Elliott, took her white third graders through that exercise the day after Martin Luther King was assassinated in 1968. She said in a talk recently that 'it's a shame we are still talking about this. Not as an example of how far we have come, but in how far we have

---

5. At the end of the first Living Legacy Award ceremony in 2006, then MNU President Ed Robinson took me aside and said that even though I was not on the stage at the presentation, I needed to realize an be pleased that I played a key part in bringing this award into being. I am pleased with this.

not come in the last fifty-five years. It should be shocking that the last reported 'confirmed' lynching of a young black man occurred in 1981 by the Ku-Klux-Klan, of nineteen-year-old Michael McDonald[6]. However, just a couple of months ago, September 2025, a black college student was found hanging from a tree in Mississippi. Officially, this was ruled a suicide. The reason these types of situations cause many to raise their eyebrows and doubt the official statement is that we realize it is quite possible that it was an actual lynching. That it is indeed possible in 2025 indicates that we continue to have racial problems such as these in the U.S.

So, when my friend and colleague left, we lost a doctoral-level professor with excellent credentials and experience in public education. That we lost a faculty member of color because of systemic racism made it a double loss. When you lose a faculty member, you also lose the professor's family's presence in the faculty community as well. By extension, this also harms the community's perception of the university. This man's wife was a school principal in a large local school district. My friend is presently an assistant superintendent in a large school district in the Kansas City, Missouri, metropolitan area. I have nothing but the highest regard for this man and his wife and am proud to call them friends. He displayed a high level of integrity by stepping into this private university, whose systemic bias was well known to him from his time as a student. As a student, he was the only black athlete among 12 to graduate. The others were kicked out or dropped out of college. In addition to his role as a professor, he was also serving as the Chief Diversity Officer when he decided to move back to the public school. I'm sure, like me, he hoped he could help change a racist system. And, in turn, significantly improve the college experiences of students of color.

In addition to the desire to get a college-level education, many, if not most, eighteen and nineteen year olds decide to attend college, and what college to attend, based on a variety of other motivations. For example, a best friend is going there, it's where their parents went to college, it's an opportunity to play sports beyond high school, and it's close to home but

---

6. 4,743 lynchings occurred in the U.S. from 1882-1968. Present day routine incarcerations of black people without legal representation is considered by many a legal substitute for lynchings. For more information you can Google *Equal Justice Initiative (EJI)*. *EJI* is an excellent source of work being done for those individuals wrongly incarcerated.

not too close. The attraction of Christian colleges is that they hold beliefs similar to those of their family, and the church they attended.

One of the most frequent student activities during the first couple of years is changing majors, which are often different from what students thought they would major in while still in high school. By design, being in the college environment facilitates this exploration of possible careers. The hope is that if the student is not really sure what they are interested in, they will discover a passion along the way. Over my twenty-five years of college teaching, I have seen this changing of majors and getting serious about one's studies hundreds of times. For Christian colleges there is also the hope that students will grow spiritually, even though they came to college for other reasons, like playing sports.

Most professors realize we only have a couple of years to get a student hooked on getting serious about learning and developing critical thinking skills. The genuine tragedy of having a student, with limited financial resources, fail out of classes was that they would be liable to miss out on an opportunity to grow intellectually and spiritually. And that they may come to believe they are not smart enough to learn. Granted, college is not for everyone. There are many paths to adulthood, and for some students, one may be no better than another.

In cases like the ones I talked about, where a student of color attends college mainly to extend their opportunity to play sports another year or two and then goes away with the assumption that they don't have what it takes to do college when they actually do, we've missed a huge opportunity. It's a shame and a tragedy when they leave with an opinion of the college that it doesn't really value and care about them because of the color of their skin.

Individuals within groups of people who are oppressed and discriminated against experience a unique brand of stress that those in the majority and in positions of power do not experience and seldom understand. This is well documented in the research. This stress comes from multiple sides. One such example is Stereotype Threat[7]. In short, this is the risk

---

7. Researchers Claude Steele and Joshua Arnson, in the mid-1990s, coined the term Stereotype Threat and the related stress.

and fear that one will confirm the negative stereotypes about one's race, gender, sexual orientation, or cultural group. This concern consumes cognitive energy and academic attention, resulting in a diminished focus on achievement. On the flip side, one black student told me that his black peers accused him of being an *Uncle Tom*[8]. Which is betraying his social and cultural allegiances. When he told his parents about this, their first question was, well, are you? Suggesting that they were also concerned with their son living up to their cultural and social allegiances. So he was in a double bind. He needed to be loyal to his heritage while doing as well as or better than his white peers in predominantly white surroundings at college. These stresses are an added burden to perform better than the feared stereotype. They often feel like they have to perform better just to be even. As I've said, there is no such thing as a level playing field. Sadly, these and several other factors are seldom taken into account by white people when supporting members of marginalized populations. These can best be accomplished by faculty members who share similar backgrounds and experiences. While educating white faculty members about these issues is truly important, having mentors who are as similar as possible to students of color is key. An effective mentor is someone who is most similar to the student: similar in race and gender, not too large a gap in age, and having coped with similar hurdles. So again, losing my friend and colleague was a tremendous loss for the university.

To the comments of white guilt: I prefer to see it as white responsibility. We only become guilty if we deflect that responsibility and look for excuses not to step up and help change the situation. White people have clearly had the power and influence in the U.S. since its inception. The ones in positions of influence always have more power to change dysfunctional systems than those who are being oppressed. Those in positions of influence have an obligation to pave the way. *To whom much is given, much is required*[9].

We must understand the correlating impact that generations of prejudice and discrimination have on non-white people. This is especially true when

---

8. Uncle Tom: a Black man considered to be excessively obedient or servile to white people.

9. Luke 12:48

this prejudice is rooted in slavery that existed only a few generations prior to the present generation

Post-traumatic stress Disorder (PTSD), as an example, can have a negative impact on children and grandchildren. Those individuals can be more susceptible to some of the same symptoms experienced by their parents and grandparents, such as sleep disturbance, problems in getting along with others, and school problems.

Similarly, Post-Traumatic Slave Syndrome (PTSS) may have a negative impact on the health and well-being of young black people, especially males.[10] When we are unaware of the potential implications of racism that was experienced by previous generations, we are ill-equipped to help young persons adequately cope with these issues when they experience them. It's easy to think that a young person has an attitude problem or only has a chip on his shoulder, when, in reality, there might be much more going on.

---

10. Jones-Everly, et.al. (2020) *Premature Deaths of Young Black Males in the United States:* In Journal o Black Studies, Vol. 51 (3), pg 251-272.

chapter 12

Weaving New and Old Threads – Back to Clinical Work

Opening the Next Chapter

Over my teaching career, I taught in the undergraduate bachelor's and graduate master's programs, developed several courses, and, with the help of a colleague, developed the Master's in Counseling program. I also held several committee chair positions and administrative positions: department chair, associate vice president of graduate studies, and associate vice president of undergraduate studies.

My last administrative role was Interim Academic Dean and Vice President for Academic Affairs (VPAA). I held this spot for twenty months. When the VVPA position was initially advertised, I decided not to apply. The first interview cycle of prospective applicants, after nine months, did not yield any desirable candidates. So I was to remain in the interim position for another academic year. At that point, because things were going pretty smoothly, a couple of key faculty members and two of the other vice presidents came to me on separate occasions and urged me to apply. This time, it was tempting to apply, which I did. However, another applicant surfaced who was working at another Nazarene institution. The search committee decided they liked him better and chose him. I finished out the academic year and assisted the new VPAA as he transitioned in.

By the time I had fulfilled this last administrative position, I knew that my personality did not fit well with higher-level administration, especially in a conservative religious denomination. Even though I received various faculty awards, such as *Faculty Member of the Year* and *Administrator of the Year*, and *Who's Who Among U.S. Teachers* voted by students, I felt like I had worn out my welcome. I believe I eventually pushed too hard, and I was no longer tolerated. Leaving the Nazarene church and becoming Episcopalian didn't help, either. I imagine this was viewed as rejection of them rather than *adding to* who I am, which I have been doing my entire life. In reality, it really was time to leave and head on to our next chapter. We've never really looked back. The timing for Joyce and me to move on was, with hindsight, perfect.

Joyce and I retired sooner than we had anticipated, Joyce from public K-5 Special Education, and me from university life. In addition to a felt lack of fit, a motivating factor was my rapidly declining hearing. It was getting more and more difficult for me to hear in the classroom and in groups. I started wearing hearing aids in my mid-forties and was told then that my hearing was similar to that of an eighty-year-old. So I guess I actually hung on pretty well.

The West Was Calling

We moved to Colorado to be close to our son, Matt, and his three kids. I returned to clinical counseling and psychological assessment work. For the first couple of years, I commuted two days a week to Colorado Springs from Parker, southeast of Denver, and two days a week in a local medical school's Internal Medicine Resident training program in Parker.

In Colorado Springs, I worked in a community counseling center that served, among others, active-duty combat soldiers stationed at Fort Carson. This was from 2010 to 2013. These soldiers were on serial deployments to Iraq and Afghanistan, many having served three to five tours, and some served up to seven. These rotations were very difficult for the soldiers and their families. They would only be home for less than

18 months before they returned to combat. Much of the counseling and therapy related to readjustment to being home, stepping in and out of family roles and soldier roles. It would take nine to twelve months to adjust to being out of a war zone and being with their families, who had continued to function without them while they were gone. By that time, they were usually getting ready to redeploy in a few months.

As an example of complex readjustment issues from being in a war zone, one soldier told me that garbage day in his housing development was always stressful. Because his wife had to be at work early in the morning, he was the one who dropped his kids off at school. But on trash day, his wife had to drop off his kids at school and be late to work. This was because it took him too long to find alternate routes that didn't require swerving around obstacles, to avoid getting too close to the garbage bags, which looked like IEDs (Innovative Explosives, shaped obstacles). The anxiety associated with this level of hypervigilance, like *having one's head on a swivel* to look out for enemy explosives, can be overwhelming. Another soldier told me he made the mistake of attending a *Taste of Denver event at* a city park. There were so many people that he couldn't keep his eyes on everyone while being sure his wife and kids were close to him, so they left only after a short while due to anxiety-related PTSD.

The price these soldiers and their families paid for war was often horrendous. Several of these soldiers were in a Wounded-Warrior-like program *and in the process of being processed out on disability.* Yet this is rarely, if ever, discussed when calculating the actual cost of war. As I said earlier, I think we're warmongers, often rushing to war as the first approach to international problems *Bully-Diplomacy.* Or, as it has been referred to, the *Quagmire* battle plans. We rush in with little or no exit strategy, and we have no thoughts as to what the follow-up steps are. I believe Congress and presidential administrations should be required to estimate, along with the cost in dollars, how many soldiers' lives will be lost and how many soldiers' families will be ruined. This is the true cost of war. In many ways, this cost of war continues for years, many years, after being discharged from the military. These are scars that are not visible to the naked eye but can last a lifetime.

It was not unusual to hear comments like, "I was very religious" or "a strong Christian when I left for Iraq, but not now." Or "I left God in Iraq." Or "I left God in Vietnam." One particular soldier was a seminary graduate and pastor when his reserve unit was deployed to Iraq during the Iraq War. When he returned from deployment, he renounced his faith altogether. The question for those who were not there or thought they knew him well was: *how could that happen?* Or they assume he must not have been a real Christian to begin with. Something as complex as apostasy has no simple answer.

My theory of what is happening to these soldiers is as follows. People raised in a particular faith often hold on to that faith in adulthood the same way they did as children. The risk here is that their religion, while sincere, is being primarily cultural: culturally Christian, culturally Jewish, culturally Baptist, and so on. As such, their faith depends on the culture of their religion—it's largely a lifestyle. Lifestyle is structured by many rules, most of which are unspoken and unconsciously assumed. These are the shoulds and oughts of life. Examples: we should accept what our pastor or other spiritual leader says without questioning; or if the pastor says something that is ill-informed then everything people like him say is wrong; if something is written in a history book in college, it's true and unquestionable; a faithful Christian should not be afraid, they should not doubt what they've been taught because it shows a lack of faith. All of this sets the stage for a form of *culture* shock.

So, for someone who returns from war and rejects their faith, we could argue that their faith may not have been examined beyond a cultural and cognitive level, as well as on an internal level, particularly when their advanced education is primarily on an intellectual level. In Buddhism, there is the belief that we all possess a Buddha Nature—an inner being. This is where enlightenment originates, it's part of our human nature. This may also be what William James was referring to as a shift of our spiritual self from the periphery to the core of who we are[1]. Granted,,we may fail to recognize this part of our nature or inner being. But it is there nonetheless, we all have the potential for enlightenment. Thus, having

---

1. James, William (1902) *The Varieties of Religious Experience,* Longmans, Green and Company

not exercised the strength of our inner being (Buddha Nature), when the external culture changes, the rules change—a person goes to war, they're in a culture that is foreign to them. This increases the risk of culture shock. Add to this the experience, directly or indirectly, of being hunted by the enemy and hunting the enemy with the object of killing a human or being killed by a human. Thus, we have a formula for the the world being turned upside down—including one's faith.

To say it another way, the cultural center of who they are becomes threatened, and their faith is threatened. So, the rules and assumptions that have governed their life no longer apply in the same way. Additionally, suppose they reject the cultural trappings of their faith, such as its rules and assumptions. In that case, it feels like they've rejected their foundational worldview, and they basically throw out the baby with the bathwater. The alternative to faith being primarily mediated by one's lifestyle, is that faith becomes mediated by more of an internal force.

It's lifestyle versus life-force. Again, William James' assertion, when we experience a religious conversion, spiritual energy shifts from the edges of who we are to the center of our identity (whether the conversion is gradual or sudden)[2]. Cultural lifestyle, is always more susceptible than a concentrated center of spiritual energy—a life force.

Post-Traumatic Stress Disorder (PTSD) in previous wars was called battle fatigue or shell shock. Although PTSD symptoms can present themselves shortly after the experience of trauma has passed, its common for deeper symptoms to not present until some later time, maybe years later- long after the actual trauma has been survived. By this time, the individual has gotten used to not talking about the traumatic event(s), or they figure they're doing just fine because the experience is in the past. The trauma has passed. They've survived, so they let down their defenses. However, those emotions have been buried alive.

For me, it happened about 15 years after I got the Air Force.

I was sitting in my dentist's chair, waiting for him to come into the room. He walked in and closed the door. He wanted to ask me a question before he started working on me. Somehow, he knew I had been in the

---

2. James, William (1902) *Varieties of Religious Experience,* Longmans, Green, & Company

Vietnam War, probably because of something in my dental history. He had been a dentist in Saigon, Vietnam, during the war. So he asked if I ever went to Vietnam war movies or watched them on TV. Almost reflexively, I answered with an emphatic no. He said that he didn't watch them either, that he didn't have the emotional tolerance for them. I agreed with him. He just wanted to know that there were other Vietnam Veterans who felt the same.

A little while later, on a Saturday morning, my teenage sons had some friends over. I had been out in the barn doing some chores. When I came into the house, the boys were watching a Sylvester Stallone war movie. Stallone's Rambo character was a Special Forces Vietnam Veteran. Rambo had been reactivated into active duty to go back to Vietnam, if I remember correctly, to bring a POW home. As mentioned earlier, I never watched Vietnam War movies, and tended to avoid war movies altogether. Neither did I give Stallone films a lot of credit for accurate realism. But I made the mistake of stopping to watch a scene for a few minutes. All of a sudden, I was overcome with grief. I hurried through the kitchen to the backyard. I must have looked funny because Joyce followed me out and asked me if I was okay. At that point, I was sobbing uncontrollably. She asked me what was wrong. I told her I had no idea. She held me, and I cried for quite a while. By talking with a psychologist, a mentor, and a good friend, I figured out what was going on with me. I was experiencing PTSD, fifteen years after I had gotten out of the Air Force in 1971.

I was not a combat soldier or in any actual danger, at least as far as we knew. But the sense that I had been involved in an immoral war had settled in. By doing my job well, keeping the equipment on the fighter jets in top order, so the pilot could get into the zone, drop bombs, and shoot up villages, and then return safely, I was a participant. This meant that I helped kill tens of thousands of people and destroyed their homes and farms. Just as important was the sense of guilt, and of loss, that I had not been home with Joyce while she was pregnant with our first son. You never get this back. All of this added to a level of depression and an edginess.

Meanwhile, my work in Colorado Springs continued to be very rewarding. In a way, I felt like I was giving back—helping soldiers who were in much more dangerous situations than I had been. They often told me they appreciated that I had been in the Vietnam War and could relate to many of their issues, like the regimentation, readjusting to family after they returned, and questioning the moral rightness of the ongoing war.

However, after a couple of years, I decided the one-way hour commute to Colorado Springs, especially in the winter months at seven thousand feet, was taking its toll. So I settled into a three-day-a-week practice at a local medical school's internal medicine clinic. As with all of my work in psychology over the last nearly fifty years, I really enjoyed this work. I saw individual clients, did cognitive status evaluations, and consulted with Internal Medicine Residents on a regular basis.

I retired fully from psychology work at the beginning of the COVID-19 epidemic in March 2020. My deafness had developed over the past 40 years. Even though I was totally deaf by then, with two cochlear implants, I could get along pretty well, especially with my ability to read lips and facial expressions. However, when people started wearing facial masks, it became impossible to understand speech. I'd been working in psychology since 1974. I continue to miss this work and the relationships I had with clients, students, and colleagues. With only a few exceptions, I've always done the work I wanted to do.

PART 6

chapter 13

Weaving New and Old Threads – Adding Buddhism

Introduction

Nothing shall separate me from the love of God in Christ Jesus[1]. We find God where we are. When we are searching for God, consciously or unconsciously, we will wake up to the spirit of God where we are. We don't have to cross the street, go to a distinct part of the city, country, or go to a different type of building. We don't have to first become a different, better person, as the old existential hymn says—*Just As I Am.*

From watching weather reports, we know that differences in upper air and lower air pressures cause blowing wind, as well as different temperatures at different altitudes. Similarly, being open to other world-views and religious perspectives can cause the wind of change to blow through our lives. These changing winds throughout the seasons of our lives winnow away the chaff that remains in the new wheat we harvest. I've been talking about adding new religious beliefs throughout my life. Even though I haven't thrown away entire points of view, there is, by necessity, a sculpting

---

1. Romans 8:35

and shaving away of debris, so to speak—central ideas and peripheral characteristics that no longer fit or belong.

As I've said, I was first exposed to the Buddhist culture during my time in Thailand, during the Vietnam War. Since this was not an active war zone, as G.I.s, we were free to move about in the area around Udorn Royal Thai Air Base. During the hours I was not working or trying to sleep in the daytime heat, I found myself, besides working out at the gym, as immersed as possible in Thai culture. I visited a couple of leprosariums during my time in Thailand, taking donations collected from the Hospitality Home and the Protestant men's group at the base chapel.

These visits really impacted me. Leprosy eventually destroys the peripheral nervous systems for grasping and "extending" fingers and toes. The loss of these basic motor functions, and sensation, can be catastrophic. The person can step on a thorn or piece of glass and not know it until it is severely infected, which, if left unchecked, becomes gangrenous resulting in amputation. Interestingly, communal bathing helps in early detection, as another person notices a lump on someone's back. The corrective surgeries that were being done to restore hand function were truly impressive. The doctors told us that the biggest need after the surgeries was trained physical and occupational therapists to help the patients develop adaptive ways to use their limbs. The creative use of reconstructive surgery involved rerouting tendons, and muscular strands from a neighboring hand or foot muscle, and nerve tissue. Essentially, their hands and feet were rewired. This was actually a significant motivator for considering Physical Therapy as a profession when I returned to college. With hindsight, the interest in working in leprosariums served as a motivator to finish my college education.

Returning To South East Asia (I Kings 19)[2]

Initially, when I left Southeast Asia in 1969, my primary goal was to leave it all behind and get on with my life. Yet over the years, I gradually came

---

2. 1 Kings 19, for many years, has been a favorite of mine in the Old Testament and has different levels of meaning to me. The prophet Elijah "thinks" he is running for his life, when he is actually running into God's presence—the Spirit of God. He finally realizes that God is not in the

to appreciate the positive impact Southeast Asia had on me. I didn't talk much about my involvement in the war. I figured there just wasn't that much to talk about. Yet I wanted Joyce to see that part of the world and meet the gentle people who lived there. Going back to Thailand became a bucket-list trip.

So, in 2019, Joyce and I took a trip to Southeast Asia. I didn't realize it when we were planning the trip that it would be like returning metaphorically to the place of my birth into adulthood, spiritually speaking. I was about to wake up to the profound impact that Buddhism and the Buddha's teachings had had on me.

We traveled for nearly a month throughout Thailand, Laos, Cambodia, and Vietnam. By this time, my hearing had steadily deteriorated into total deafness. I had one cochlear implant, which was a true game-changer. However, I still relied heavily on reading facial expressions and contextual hearing. I often rely on Joyce to clarify what is said to me. Due to being deaf, a primary concern when I travel is having a guide whose English is clear enough for me to understand. We learned of a tour agency based in Ho Chi Min City (Saigon), Vietnam, that provided one-to-one tours. We stressed the importance that the English spoken by our guides be as clear and without strong accents as much as possible. It turned out I could understand much of what they said when I looked them straight in the eye. Joyce, as always, helped fill in the blanks of my understanding.

We started in Bangkok. Our guide met us at the airport and took us in a comfortable van to our hotel. Before I actually thought about what I was saying, I told Joyce it was great to be back." Throughout the first several days, I was overwhelmed with emotion, often feeling close to tears, which was unexpected. On the second day in Bangkok, we visited typical tourist sites, such as Buddhist Temples, and took a boat tour through a housing region with floating homes. These houses were essentially shanties. Americans would consider these houses slums: laundry hanging over porch rails and cute, adorable, but poor-looking children.

---

spectacular things (earthquakes, wind storms, fire) like others have believed were signs of God. Now he has to listen to the gentle things, a gentle blowing of the wind. When he finally listens he is instructed to "go back the way he had come from" and let go of the past, the traditional way of seeing.

As we were making our way down the waterway, a Buddhist Monk paddled his way, going in the opposite direction. He was picking up food that had been placed on small platforms attached to the porches. People leave food on the porches each day for monks to pick up for their daily sustenance. The people we saw looked just like the people who were bombed and shot during the Vietnam War. Some two hundred thousand Vietnamese were killed during the war. At one point, we were up on top of a Buddhist temple building and were looking down on all the people in the streets. I was struck by how much I felt like I was a part of them, and they were a part of me.

That night at dinner at a sidewalk cafe, Joyce and I were talking about the day. I was suddenly overcome with weeping. I couldn't even speak for a while. Joyce just held my hand across the table. As I regained my composure, I told her how angry I was at the U.S. government for using me and thousands of other young men and women to commit such immoral acts in the war. I apologized to her again, for being gone during her pregnancy and the birth of Scott. Even though I had been drafted against my will, I still felt and feel responsible for being gone for that most crucial year, as well as participating in those atrocities. I've heard the arguments of family and friends that I have actually opened up to, that there was nothing I could have done. It was the decision of our government in the 1960s. However, that doesn't really help much. I realize they can't relate to what I'm feeling about all of that.

After a couple of days in Bangkok, we flew up-country to Udon Thani, where my Air Force base was—specifically Udorn Royal Thai Air Force Base. Each time we flew to a new stop during our time in Southeast Asia, a local guide would meet us who lived in that area. Udorn Air Base is about fifteen minutes by jet aircraft from Hanoi. Udorn was the launching place for military operations that the U.S. denied doing until recently, in Laos, Cambodia, and north of the demilitarized zone in Vietnam. My emotions had begun to settle, though not entirely. Udon Thani had morphed from a small village to a city of one million over the last 50 years.

Throughout the rest of our month in Southeast Asia, I became increasingly aware of how much this part of the world was a part of who I am. Without realizing it, I had left a part of myself, of my soul, in

Thailand—in gentle Buddhist Thailand. After touring northern Thailand on the Myanmar border and a small portion of western Laos, we eventually flew out of Bangkok on our way to Phnom Penh, Cambodia. I realized how much I was leaving, again, a part of me in Thailand. I was sad to leave in several ways—quite a contrast to fifty years before.

I titled this chapter "Adding Buddhism." Earlier in my life, I would have thought one had to move totally away from one thing to take on another. But for me, it really has been adding-to, adding Buddhism to my Christian faith. My spirituality is an accumulation of studying and adopting various creeds, rather than completely abandoning a single set of beliefs. There is enough room, breadth, and depth of spirit to accommodate the lifetime of experiences that we have as humans. This is part of the same pattern of spiritual growth I began back when I first went off to college at nineteen. Or much younger at seven when, contrary to my Grandpa Oscar's protest, I was adding the validity of evolution to my understanding of how the world works. When I was stationed at Udorn, a Buddhist Monk, Sawan, frequented the Hospitality Home in downtown Udon Thani. He liked to practice his English and enjoyed meeting us G.I.s. Some of the G.I.s that gathered there were very evangelical and often talked to Sawan about converting to Christianity. He finally said, at one point, that he believed he could accept Christianity——to believe in Jesus the Christ, but that he would also remain a Buddhist——a Christian Buddhist. He was accepting something new to add to who he was. At the time, that sounded like a failed compromise. That he needed to reject his orange robes and grow his hair out. Now I get that. Jesus and Buddha did not just say the same things in different ways. They clearly said different things, but not necessarily in competition with each other. *Most religious traditions are not cumulative. They reject an outworn creed when they move on to a new stage. The ability to accommodate rather than reject older beliefs has a very practical outcome.*[3]

So, I've had an appreciation for Buddhism for the majority of my adult life. Recently, I've also been reading the works and taking an online

---

3. Nagler, Michael, N. (2009) *A Religion for Modern Times*, pg 308-309. In Easwaran, Eknath (2009) *The Upanishads*, Nilgiri

course in Franciscanism by Richard Rohr. Rohr's writing served as a ballast for me during my early exploration of Buddhism[4] His Franciscan teaching and writing blends and easily incorporates Eastern Religious beliefs, such as Buddhism. The first book I read by Rohr, twenty-five years ago, was "Everything Belongs." This book reinforced my journey of inter-religious integration. Rohr described a scene in Jerusalem at Christmas time. Christmas Carols are being sung at a Christian church, prayers are being prayed at the Wailing Wall. A call for evening prayers is being made over loudspeakers from the Islamic Mosque. It's a regular cacophony of sounds that raises an important question, says Rohr: "It's never been a question asking if God could bring peace on earth. The real question is, 'can we?'"

As I've mentioned before, this is a spiritual journey or pilgrimage for me. At this point, I would describe myself as a Christian who has significant Buddhist leanings. Buddhism is a positive influence on my spirituality. Eighty years of being a Christian is a long time. I've been consciously appreciative of Buddhism for the last 50 years, but only actively studying it over the previous 15+ years. Without that influence, I'm not sure I would consider myself a Christian any longer. I've found Buddhism to fill key gaps in my spirituality and philosophy of life. In many ways, at this point, I'm thinking of Buddhism as part of the back-story of the ministry of Jesus. Developmentally, it seems that Jesus picked up where Buddha left off. Buddha discovered that, as humans, we all have the potential to be enlightened. To become self-aware. This then sets the stage for recognizing the Spirit of God, which is all around us and in us and is what Jesus brought to us. I suppose I'm a *Modern Buddhist,* believing in many of the Buddha's teachings. Buddhist philosophy makes good psychology and is consistent with much of how the mind works— good Existential Psychology, good Cognitive Behavior Psychology, good Humanistic Psychology, good Positive Psychology. Regular practices like meditation and contemplation can lead to enlightenment. All humans have the potential for this. It's in our nature. Buddha taught his followers to be critical thinkers, never accepting concepts uncritically, and to learn

---

4. Father Richard Rohr is a Franciscan Priest who established the Center for Action and Contemplation, in Albuquerque, New Mexico

Receiving blessing Cambodian Buddhist Nun

to be present in the moment, apart from the past and from worrying about the future. This is a continuous process.

I especially like the emphasis that Pieris places on the two-fold aspect of Christ and Buddha[5] The first being that Buddha's teaching focuses on an interior liberation, an emotional and psychological freeing. Second, Jesus' demand for a 'structural change in human relationships'. In current parlance, *walking the talk*. Jesus's radical demand is, of course, what eventually led to Jesus' crucifixion, a punishment reserved for the lawless and terrorists.

To those who have gotten this far in this book, especially my grandkids, I hope you will keep an open mind throughout your lives. If something new seems reasonable to you and yet runs counter to what you have

---

5. Pieris, A, in Drew, Rose (2011) *Buddhist and Christian: An Exploration of Dual Belonging,* pg 100. Routledge

believed in other parts of your life, at least put that something on the back burner, so to speak. Over time, the contradictions will either melt away as you continue to consider the two almost as different parts of the same truth. Or one or the other will become obviously false. It's okay to hold two contradictory things in your mind while you allow time and experience to help you sort things out. It's okay to say you don't know how two or more logical things fit together.

Buddha Nature

All humans have a Buddha Nature, the potential to be enlightened. Whether we exercise that nature to become enlightened is another matter. But as humans, it's a choice as to whether we cultivate that nature; we are capable of it.

Christianity's core, as it is practiced today in the West, is centered on an ideological existential core of being, which rapidly morphs tangentially into classifications: Catholic or Protestant, Baptist or Methodist. Christians, down through history, have fought wars over these classifications, drowned people in rivers, enslaved humans, and banned classes of people from worshiping together. Sadly, it's what we Christians believe and how we identify ourselves. Believing that Jesus is the Son of God and accepting him into our hearts/souls is the starting point. However, throughout history up to today, if you don't believe this exactly like I do, then we are apt to engage in a Holy War of sorts.

Christianity's premise is that Right Belief comes in from the outside, from God into us. Once this is established, Right Behavior springs from those beliefs. Buddhism, on the other hand, is centered on achieving enlightenment from that which is already a part of our (Buddhist) nature. Then, Right Behavior emerges and asks questions: how do we stop the suffering of all sentient beings; how do we bring peace to the world we live in, and into the world in general? How best can we feed the poor and stop violence and gun-related murders, which the rest of the world identifies as the very nature of the U.S.? How do we go about stopping or preventing the marginalization of human beings based on any number of self-centered traits and differences in personality: color of skin, families that people are born into, sexual orientation? Buddhism believes that Right Beliefs will develop from the enlightenment that attempts to resolve these things. We already have the ability to *discover* how to solve these issues. It's part of our Buddha-Nature, how we are born as human beings.

Inner-Being and Inner-Connectedness

A central premise of Buddhism is the concept of Inter-Being. That an internal being, or emptiness, already exists in us. It's the idea that we really only exist in relationship with others. (This is what St Francis of Assisi also believed and taught.) This is where spirit energy exists—a dynamic energy that is the environment in which we live. Like the water a fish lives in and swims freely. For Christians, this is where God is. Even though it runs counter to much of what rugged western individualism would have us believe, we can't be described as stand-alone individuals, but only as we exist in relationship, inter-connectedness, with the rest of God's creation. The emptiness that exists within me is indeed empty, without interaction with the rest of creation. I don't exist without that inner-connectedness. Jesus' prayer to the Father in John 17:21 that they "will all be one [in the future] as you and I are one" (in the present). This idea is stressed in the New Testament teaching on Christian fellowship: all members of one body are equal, each part is as important as the others, and each part is as crucial as the others. Speaking of the quality of this relationship, the New Testament writer, Peter, remarks, "how much Jesus' followers *love* one another."[6] One can tell they are Christians by their love [for each other]. This seems to have been all but lost in present-day American Christianity, especially Evangelical/Conservative Christian circles in the U.S.

Buddhism takes this idea of inter-being even further: this love for others includes all of Creation, whether the other person belongs to a Christian denomination, is a follower of one of the other big three religions—Islam, Christianity, and Judaism—or Buddhism, Hinduism, Atheism, and so on. In Buddhism, this love and inner connection applies to all of sentient creation, as well as respect and care for vegetation,

---

6. I Peter 1:22-2:3

the earth, etcetera. This interrelatedness is similar to the web, which has become an expected part of the internet. Within moments of searching the web for a book on a specific subject or a particular woodworking tool, I receive ads on Facebook and texts about several options I hadn't found during my initial search. Similar to gently pushing one part of a spider web, a vibration of energy is communicated to a distant portion of another part of the web. This is how we are all interconnected with each other. This is how we are created.

I love a line in a song by Steven Stills about his relationship with his wife: "... *there is no separating me and you.*"[7] To define me, you would have to include the impact that Joyce has on me and describe her as well. I have two sons and six grandchildren. They are each unique, and as such, each one is my favorite. To define me, you would have to include the impact that each of these young people has on who I am. In her book, *The Company They Keep*, Glyer relates how one of the Inklings, a group of writers including C.S. Lewis and J.R.R. Tolkien, describes the death and loss of one of their members. Not only do they miss this member, but they also miss what he brought out in each of the other individual members that no one else can bring out in the same way.[8]

Interconnectedness is more than just knowing that someone else exists in your space, like a neighbor you wave to occasionally. It's knowing on a deeper level, a transcendent level, a "knowing by which all things are known", in a way that our very being and actions are transformed[9]. In a very real sense, I become identified with her/him, and she/he with me. The known becomes the knower. The knower becomes the known. Seeing through the symbolism of a ritual, such as a wedding, to its inner core of meaning. We become one. Our very identity is changed.

---

7. Steven Stills of *Crosby, Stills, Nash, & Young* fame

8. Glyer, Diana Pavlac (2007) *The Company They Keep: C.S. Lewis and J.R.R. Tolkien: Writers in Community.*

9. Nagler, Michael, N (2007) *Afterward: A Religion for Modern Times,* In Easwarn, Eknath *The Upanishads* Nigiri Press

Suffering

Suffering is one of the four Noble Truths of Buddhism. We all suffer in various ways throughout our lives. Pain, be it mental, emotional, or physical, is part of our human condition. Pain alerts us to avoid repeating harmful actions toward ourselves and others. We accidentally touch a hot stove and we learn to be more careful. Suffering associated with pain is similar to the goofy uncle who shows up at family gatherings he comes with the territory. We suffer from the effects of learned and conditioned evolution. Suffering is not only first nature but also second nature. The Bible says not to be surprised when fiery trials come our way, *as if it is unusual.* In other words, it is part of life.[10]

That actual suffering may be as much a conditioned, learned response to pain as it is separate from pain was a key learning point in my early days working in psychology. My first exposure to this concept came when I worked with Dr. Snow in the VA. Although we may have chronic pain, suffering really is optional, at the very least it's a matter of degree, like on a scale from zero to ten. The goal in Behavioral Pain Management is to remove the suffering from chronic pain. Yes, I can be in pain, but suffering—being totally inactive, removing myself totally from social and family interaction, never going to a concert again—can be learned to be only a side issue. Pain and suffering do not have to go hand in hand. Eliminating suffering from the pain we experience is a central goal of Buddhism.

No Self

No [permanent] self really exists. At any point in time, this is me now. But it will not be exactly who I am tomorrow, next week, next month. The self is always transitory. The self is the result of what has happened prior to this moment and will be different next week. Who we will be is the result of what happens now, tomorrow, and so on. Who I am is also affected by how I react to the situation I'm in now. This is both a Buddhist principle and a psychological principle. The self consists of five

---

10. 1 Peter 4:12

interacting elements of consciousness: 1) volition (motivation), our will, 2) perception, 3) feelings, 4) body (physical form), and 5) consciousness. These are constantly interacting with each other. At no point in time can I say that I'm only my perception, or only volition, or only feelings, and so on. My 'self' is the interaction of these elements; self is constantly in flux.

Trying harder and harder to cling to what we are, what we've achieved, or what we crave is like trying to hold on to smoke. Believing our accomplishments or our failures are who we are, what we've accomplished, or what we desire, clinging to those things is what causes suffering. Peace comes from being in the now and mindfully being aware of only the now. Not clinging to what was or obsessing about what will be in the future. If we try to cling to our view of ourselves we suffer: we become anxious, depressed, obsessed, fearful, and the list goes on. In Buddhism, the urge to cling to who we are today and to what we possess is the source of pain and suffering. This craving keeps us on guard against perceived threats that may try to take away the things that we think satisfy us and keeps us on the hunt for things that will alleviate what we think is ailing us. If we can achieve this level of education, secure that position, own that car, and be liked by that person, we will be happy and satisfied. However, following the attainment of that which we have thirsted for, our brains are built to ask what have you done for me lately, and to want the new satisfaction all over again. Meditation helps us transcend this by helping us find satisfaction with who and what we are now. The Apostle Paul said that he had become satisfied with whatever state he found himself in.

It can be both a strong and subtle temptation to hold onto what we have been and let it define who we are. It's easy to let both the negative and positive aspects of our past define who we are as we go into the future: proud of what we are from the past, and afraid of who we don't want to continue to be in the future. Examples: being a star athlete in college or an academic scholar. I know an individual with a PhD in nuclear science who insists that the neighborhood kids call him "doctor." While it's understandable that this fiftyish-year-old man is proud of his accomplishments, he fails to see that he can be so much more by being a kind neighbor and caring father in his neighborhood. On the flip side, it can also be easy for some people to allow the more destructive and painful parts of who we were to be the basis of their identity—a victim of abuse, a debilitating injury. People with chronic illness can get so used to seeing themselves as the disease that they fail to see the strengths they possess. To describe oneself as 'a diabetic', rather than 'having diabetes', can reinforce this weakness in their body and allow it to overshadow many other strengths that they possess. To be able to say they have a disease, the disease doesn't have them. One goal in rehabilitation psychology is to help a person who has been the victim of an accident that has left them partially paralyzed move beyond that traumatic event. One of the rewarding aspects of working in physical rehabilitation is seeing individuals rise above the trauma they experienced and go on to live satisfying and productive lives, despite the challenges life has brought their way. I'm not suggesting that we ignore natural and traumatic limitations. But what I am suggesting is that we accept and acknowledge limitations which may come our way, and then learn to cope positively with the limitations that are there, learn to cope positively with them, and do the very best we can within those limitations. In many ways, this is what normal, healthy aging is about. As we age, certain limitations are just part of the process. Making adjustments and staying as active as possible is part of healthy aging.

Buddhism stresses the importance of living in the present. While grieving our losses as they come along is essential, the more we hang on to those losses by perseverating and clinging to our sadness over the loss and wishing we had what we had before, the more we get stuck in the past. Sadness should be a temporary state. Then we adapt to what today brings. This is one of the aspects of Rehabilitation Psychology, specifically coping with permanent or long-term loss. Accepting that the life we've known up to this point is over. It's time to see what our life is like now in this new phase. I've long been impressed with rehabilitation patients who experience significant loss, as well as those who experience more common loss, like divorce, loss of a job, or death of a friend or loved one. As human beings, we are amazingly resilient and can, over time, recover from what life brings our way.

As I mentioned earlier, I'm totally daaf at this point in my life. It's an *acquired hearing loss*. I didn't really notice it when I first got out of the Air Force after working around jet aircraft for three years; the onset was so gradual that I didn't notice it until the mid-1980s, about fifteen years following my time in the Air Force. A psychology client, who was profoundly hard of hearing, was describing how his hearing aids worked for him and the difference they made. He mentioned the ringing in his ears and difficulty hearing in noisy situations. I thought, oh my, that's me. Because the loss had been so gradual, I had, without realizing it, made adjustments along way.

I didn't think much more about it at the time. It wasn't until I took a full-time teaching position, a couple of years later, that I realized how hard it was for me to hear students in larger classrooms with poor acoustics. These larger rooms had a lot of echo. So I made an appointment with a hearing clinic. They asked me if I had ever been around loud noises?? They told me my hearing, at forty-six years of age, was equivalent to that of an eighty-year-old. So I got my first hearing aid and assumed that I was fixed. However, each time I went in for a yearly follow-up appointment, adjustments had to be made due to the continually declining hearing. An audiologist told me this was actually a good time to be going deaf, due to the research and development of increasingly sophisticated hearing aids. I didn't pay much attention to the "deaf" part, but was happy they were always able to make adjustments. But when I was honest with myself, I knew deafness was on the horizon. Eventually, I got my first cochlear implant in 2011 at sixty-five.

There were several points along the way when I had to recognize that I could no longer function at certain levels of hearing. Having to stop teaching, because I couldn't understand students' questions, was hard for me to swallow. Each point along the way was challenging to accept at the time. But I was usually able to take deep breaths and then find what I needed to do to adapt. As we age, we're all constantly changing and adapting. There's no such thing as a stable, permanent self, physically or mentally. Our essence, our self is never a permanent entity. Permanence is an illusion.

Another Buddhist belief which parallels the "no permanent self" is the concept of No-Self. This is the belief that no "one being is a totally isolated individual". We are not individuals in the sense that none of us is able to stand totally alone. Everyone is interrelated. We're obviously interconnected with immediate family members, extended family, and close friends. But we are also Inter-Connected with the people in line with us at the grocery check-out, and with the checker. With people pan-handling at freeway exits. With the mechanic that we employ to work on our car. With the receptionist in our doctor's office. In this way, if we are genuinely able to see all others in this way, I suspect we will rarely want to go to war because those that we see as our enemy are actually intercon-nected, they are us. Essentially, they are us.

The way I understand my being at this point is that I'm a Christian who has taken on many aspects of Buddhism. That's the type of Christian I am. Buddhism addresses what is, by nature, within us. The goal is to awaken and become enlightened about what already exists within me. A primary goal of a clinical psychologist is to set the stage for clients and students to discover what already exists within them. Christianity, through the person of Jesus, brings this natural part of me in touch with the Spirit of God. The two work in tandem, facilitating each other.

Connected To All Creation

Over dinner several years ago, while talking gingerly around current po-litical views with some long-time conservative Christian friends of ours, they made it abundantly clear, in no uncertain terms, that they were not Greenies by which they meant they were definitely not environmentalists. As they talked, they implied that they had risen above, focusing on the environment. As environmentalists, if we were "save the whalers, there were obvious questions in their minds about the depth and sincerity of our Christian faith. People who are Greenies have gotten sidetracked from the true Gospel of Jesus. Our friends had let the politicization of environmental issues taint their faith. In Buddhism, love and care for the environment are part of the Buddhist nature.

Peace

In Buddhism, there is no such thing as a just war. While pacifists, or an-ti-war individuals and groups like the Amish, exist in Christianity, they are viewed as outliers, on the fringe at best. Dorothy Day, founder of the Catholic Worker in the early and middle of the last century, was jailed for peacefully sitting in the way of police in demonstrations against war——specifically the Vietnam War.[11] Presently in the U.S., if such people are considered Christian at all, they certainly are not seen as patriotic by many Christians. It is assumed that they don't love their country and are suspected of being Communists or Socialists. That there is no just war is one aspect I've added from Buddhism to my faith with roots in Christianity.

Our Buddhist Nature

Another way to consider my combination of spiritual beliefs that I'm coming to understand, is pointed out by Paul Knitter: that we all possess a Buddha Nature, just as we possess a Christ Nature.[12] Buddha teaches a broader picture of a divine spiritual energy and enlightenment. Since we all possess a Buddhist-like Nature, we are all capable of enlightenment. Christ teaches the specifics of how to live out this principle. Adding Buddhism to my Christianity is like adding the inner-being part of who I am. Jesus picks up where Buddha left off. I'm finding in Buddhism what I haven't found in Christianity, particularly in American Conservative Christianity.

Buddha's teaching focuses primarily on the existential question of suffering: how to alleviate the suffering that plagues humankind. How do we stop the exclusion of people to the margins of society—people of color, the poor, LGBTQA+, peaceniks? Granted, I have conservative Christian friends and associates who echo these concerns. However, in Buddhism, these issues are primary. Buddhism, as I have experienced so far, does not appear to concern itself with a political party, ethnicity, or sexual orientation of others.

---

11. Forest, Jim (2011) *Biography of Dorthy Day,* Orbis Books

Mayfield, D.L. (2022) *Unruly Saint: Dorthy Day's Radical Vision and It's Challenge for our Times,* Broadleaf Books

12. Knitter, Paul (2009) *Without Buddha I Could Not be a Christian,* Oneworld Publications. Paul is Professor of Theology, World Religions and Culture at Union Seminary in New York City

In Sum, at Least For Now

Even though these and other issues mentioned here are said by some to exist within Christianity, they seem to me to exist only in certain specific individuals, if at all, or in specialized groups: maybe in some missionaries, some clergy, or other sub-groups. They do not seem to be part of the goals of Christian living for the vast majority of people who identify as Christ's followers. I'm certainly not an academically trained theologian or historian. But from my experiences, the studying I have done as a layperson, the company I have kept ninety percent of my life, and the academic training I've mentioned, that I've gained from Buddhism appear to be rare exceptions in Christianity rather than the rule. At least in Christianity, which I'm familiar with.

As long as I can remember, in Christianity there has been a works-versus-faith debate. According to John's gospel, doing the truth is more important than believing the truth. In Knitter's writing, he cites Thich Nhat Hanh, 'the truth can never be made absolute. There will always be other truths, more profound truths, or we come to understand truth differently.[13]

Central to Buddhism are the Four Noble Truths: 1. Everyone suffers or experiences dissatisfaction; 2. Craving or clinging, rigidly, to what we believe is "our right" is the cause of this suffering; 3. There's a way to eliminate suffering; 4. Cultivating the Noble Enlightened Path can end suffering.

The Noble Enlightened Path is: Wise View, Wise Intention, Wise Speech, Wise Action, Wise Livelihood, Wise Effort, Wise Mindfulness, and Wise Concentration. Mahayana Buddhism, which includes the practice of Zen meditation and mindfulness, considers psychological bondage to be the result of patterns of thought. These patterns of thought lead to automatic or reflexive thinking about self and others. This is a mis-knowing and deluded consciousness that leads to conditions such as poor self-esteem, depression, anxiety, and a host of other psychological problems.[14]

---

13. Ibid

14. Drew, Rose (2011) *Buddhist and Christian? An exploration of dual belonging,* page 116; Routledge Publishers, New York, NY

It's this straightforward assertion of Buddhism that is so appealing to me. It's good psychology.

Over the last thirty-five years, I've written consistently about how I see the integration of Christian faith, and psychology. To see the relationships between psychological principles and Christian beliefs requires interpretation of those Christian scriptures, as well as psychological research. Integrating Christian Spirituality, with good psychology, involves a measure of interpretation on both sides of the equation. Further, this occurs within the cultural contexts in which I've lived. Not unexpectedly, as I've continued studying and grown older some of those conclusions have changed.

Buddhism refers to this evolving truth as *contextual* truth as contrasted with *ultimate* truth. As contexts have changed, these interpretations have changed, and as such, have been subject to debate. Buddhism's Noble Enlightened Path doesn't need so much interpretation. It seems self-evident, at least to me. So, as I've said earlier, Jesus' teachings, such as the Beatitudes in the Sermon on the Mount, build on the Buddha's groundwork. [15]

I certainly don't intend this as a sermon. But my reticence to preach seems to be a result of my developing personality over my adult years, and is reinforced in me as I identify more with Buddhism. This is part of what has made me an effective psychologist, professor, and loving husband, father, and grandfather. Although I've never been reluctant to express my views, especially when asked, I'm relatively shy about proclaiming unsolicited opinions and points of view. I'm sure there are several exceptions, with the most notable exceptions have to do with overt and covert racism, our current treatment of asylum seekers and the homeless, gun violence, and issues related to the safety of my family.

Part of what has drawn me, beyond my conservative Christian faith has been what I see as a present-day, 500 plus years in the making, American Christianity whose roots are very Eurocentric. These Eurocentric origins mask and delude the Gospel of Jesus. While many like to assert that the U.S. was founded on Christian values, I understand and read our history

---

15. Matthew 5:3-10

differently. The Eurocentric roots of the U.S. are very much reflected in a colonialist and white superiority complex. Even though our forefathers talked about the importance of religious freedom as a basis for the U.S., it seems we have to fight continually against the conservative tendencies to turn us into a Christian (particularly a Conservative Christian) nation, rather than a religiously free nation. Just ask your Muslim, Jewish, Buddhist, or Atheist friends and acquaintances.

Occasionally, very occasionally, someone will ask what led me to think a particular way, such as adding Buddhism to my faith. Then, when I've attempted to explain, I often get no response, or an attempt to convince me that my views are wrong. In my memory, only once or twice has a Christian asked me what it is that attracts me to Buddhism. Nor do I recall anyone saying that, given my respect for you as a thoughtful and reasonably intelligent person, I should give this some consideration and accept it about you.

What you have read here is clearly a work in progress, an ongoing pilgrimage. I started writing the first version in the fall of 2023, and this revision in Spring of 2025. At some point, I realize I'll need to say this is enough for now. But, in summary for now, I'm seeing Christianity and Buddhism as almost parallel tracks, each important to the other. Each saying something quite different but complementary. Each pointing to the ultimate truth.

What I have written here speaks of me and no one else. The frustrations I've talked about are my frustrations and should not be taken as "shoulds" for others. If some of what I've said speaks to you and encourages you to think differently or deeper, leading to new insights, so much the better. Over the last fifty years, about the time I've been convinced that a particular religious perspective or dogma is clearly wrong or misguided, I come upon someone who has found their experiences of that perspective to be the opposite of mine, and that perspective has turned out to be life-giving for them. I will re-state, however, that issues that are destructive to our society: racism, prevalence of gun violence, domestic violence, and marginalization of people due to race, religious creeds, and sexual orientation are unequivocally wrong regardless of a person's religious rationale or political justification.

Buddhism places emphasis on knowing oneself and learning to live in the moment. This idea of living in the moment, in the here and now, is also a psychological principle that emphasizes the importance of understanding that the past is truly gone. There's nothing we can do about it except maybe learn from it. Forgiveness of self and others is a crucial tool for this. The future is always not here yet. Although we can and should plan for the future, those plans need to be fluid. Life is full of unpredictable twists and turns.

chapter 14

EPILOGUE—Fall 2025

Joyce and I are living the retired life in Parker, Colorado, on the southern edge of the Metropolitan Denver area. We live a mile from Matt and his three kids. Matt is a single dad, and as such, makes us so very proud of the dad he is and his ability to juggle everything that entails being a single parent. Palin, his oldest, just finished her final semester of her bachelor's degree at Denver University. She is planning to begin a master's degree in the fall and then go on to become a Physician Assistant. She played tennis in high school and went to the State Tournament for three years. One year, the state tournament was canceled due to COVID-19. Phoenix graduated from high school in spring 2024, and played one year of ice hockey at Western Washington University. He graduated from the Fire Fighter's Academy in December. He always adds life to wherever he is. Penn, short for Pennington, is a junior in high school. Penn has tried his hand and has been successful at hockey and at volleyball; however, he has settled on golf, partially because golf is more cerebral. He is a natural athlete. I'm predicting he may well become the philosopher of the family. He was inducted into the National Honor Society for High School students last Spring. It is a true blessing to live so close to them and to see them regularly.

In the spring, Tony, my sister Dawn's eldest, moved here to Colorado and stayed with us for a few months. It was really fun to have him with us. He lives about twenty minutes from us.

We have become hockey fans. The Denver University Hockey Team has won 10 NCAA national championships. More than any other university hockey program in the country. So going to their games is really exciting. We have season tickets with Matt.

Scott and his wife, Bahar, live in New Jersey with their three kids. Zain is fourteen, and in Boy Scouts with plans to become an Eagle Scout. Noor, Noony, is twelve. Noony is on track to become an activist and has put together several fundraisers for animal shelters. Last year she got a spot on a City Council meeting agenda in Short Hills, NJ. Her concern was that, as a Muslim, the public schools needed to recognize one of the Muslim holidays with no school, just as they do for Hanukkah and Christmas. She is also the family's artist. Sami is nine and has taken on the role of keeping everyone on their toes.

While Scott was paying back the Army for medical school, he did a tour in Kosovo at a UN base, and later did a tour in Baghdad, Iraq. Much of his time in Baghdad was spent working in the ER on Iraqi and U.S. soldiers. This was during the hot time in the Iraq War. They often had to do surgery while wearing flak vests and helmets. Scott and Bahar are both dermatologists. Scott has a couple of private practice offices in and around Princeton. Bahar teaches and is the Medical Director of the Dermatology Clinic at Rutgers University Medical School. We try to see the New Jersey family three to four times a year. They come here to Colorado every February to spend time with us in the mountains, where they all ski.

Joyce and I travel as much as we can. We went on a Danube and Rhine river cruise from Amsterdam to Budapest in the summer of 2025. We're trying to figure out what we will do for our sixtieth anniversary in March of 2026.

Joyce continues to have much more energy than I do. Her hobbies include reading, piano lessons, yard work during the non-snowy months, watercolor painting, and walking a few miles three days a week. Most of our neighbors know who Joyce is. She loves to bake and frequently takes an extra batch of cookies or other baked goods to them.

Joyce is the kindest person I know. Her kindness and love permeate every relationship she has, including with her students when she was teaching. One of my favorite stories of her days of teaching took place when we lived in Puyallup, Washington. She was teaching second grade in the Bethel School District, south of Tacoma. Her school was located a quarter-mile from a bus route that started about twenty-five miles away in downtown Tacoma. So people who needed affordable housing would have transportation and could make it into Tacoma and back for work. Ninety percent of the students in her school were eligible for free and reduced lunch.

Early in the school year, she received a request over the intercom to visit the administrative office. She was getting a new student. She went to meet her new boy, Matt. He looked disheveled and didn't make eye contact with her. The principal informed her that he had already attended two other district schools and had been expelled. This was his final opportunity before being banned from the district altogether. At his previous school, he was involved in a fight and threw a desk at another student. (Remember, this is second grade.)

Shortly after she had shown Matt his desk, it was time for recess. In Western Washington, it rains frequently. The school had a large covered play area, but the ground still got wet. As the other children were getting their coats on to go outside, Matt pulled a note from his pocket and gave it to Joyce. The note had obviously been written by Matt, even though he had signed his mom's name. Joyce's first thought was that he had been in her class less than an hour and had already forged a note from his mother. The note said that his mother was requesting that Matt not go out for recess. Joyce asked Matt why he could not go outside. Without making eye contact, he explained that his socks were wet from walking to school and didn't want to get them wetter. Matt showed her his shoes. Both shoes had holes, and on one, the sole was barely attached to the toe and flopped when he walked. Indeed, his feet were soaking wet. Matt explained he had had to walk to school because the bus came before he had made the snack for his younger sibling in kindergarten.

Once the rest of the kids had gone out for recess, Joyce had him stand on a piece of paper so she could trace his foot. At lunch, she went to Walmart and bought two pairs of shoes that were the size of the tracing. She didn't whether he knew how to tie his shoes, so one pair had Velcro closures. When she got back to school, she pulled Matt out of the lunchroom and told him she wanted to trade him one of the new pairs of shoes for his old pair. He immediately selected the ones without the Velcro.

For the rest of the day in class, he couldn't help but look down at his new shoes. At the afternoon recess, she noticed he was challenging other boys to a race around the play area. Matt became Joyce's chief defender for the rest of the school year. The only fights he got into were when someone said something negative about Mrs. Henning.

A few days later, Joyce learned why Matt had written the note from his mother and signed it. His mom was illiterate and couldn't read or write. We have the pair of shoes with one sole barely hanging on in our home office. I've told this story, and held up the shoes, to students in the graduate counseling program as an example that everyone has things going on in their lives which other people know nothing about. These things might very well account for other different problems on the surface.

I enjoy reading. Since retirement, I've taken up woodworking, which includes wood burning. I often participate in an art show in Parker. Several years ago, I had a nasty crash on my bike and broke my pelvis and tailbone. Before that, I had regular semi-crashes resulting in road rashes and bruises. Upon breaking my pelvis, my family finally became pretty insistent that I not ride a two-wheeler anymore.

So, I got a recumbent trike. It was assumed that the trike was more difficult to crash, but I proved that assumption wrong within a month or so of getting it. It's not as far to the ground, though. As the mechanic was straightening out the rear-derailer, which I bent on the crash, he reminded me that there are two types of cyclists: those who have crashed and those who are going to crash. I ride twenty to twenty-five-plus miles three times a week when the snow has melted from the local bike trail. Until my most recent knee replacement surgery, I rode in at least one charity ride each summer. The longest ride was in Oregon. I rode up to Crater Lake and back down—63 miles. I'm afraid the chapter of long rides may well be closed. I'll have to see.

Charity Ride 2019

chapter 15

Changing the world I live in.

Christianity and Buddhism talk about the importance of contemplation and action. Although the road to these two is arrived at differently, along different paths in the two faiths, and the order of importance is different, the end result is the same. They seem to me to be two sides of the same coin. In a mature spirituality, you can't have one without the other. What follows here are some examples of issues with which I am passionate and, as such, guide my actions, which spring from my meditations and contemplation. My actions include regular financial support, who and what I vote for, and, when given the opportunity, what I speak up about.

SYSTEMIC RACISM: I've probably said enough about that already.

LGBTQA+: After reading Thomas and Alexa Oord's book, "Why the Church of the Nazarene Should be Fully Affirming," I wrote an essay that appeared on the Loving Nazarene's website. The essay regards concerns over LGBTQA+ youth who lack support from their church communities. The lack of support and acceptance from their communities further isolates developing teens. This lack of acceptance and support increases the likelihood of self-harm and suicidal ideation.

GUN VIOLENCE: This issue is directly related to our suffering as humans. During our time in Europe, while teaching at European Nazarene College (EuNC), I would occasionally hear U.S. exchange students commenting about how comfortable Europeans seemed to be with nudity, occasionally seeing a billboard sign with a nude woman. European student, on the other hand, would comment about how comfortable the U.S. was with violence, specifically gun violence, expressing fear about visiting the U.S. due to their perceived danger. That was twenty-five years ago. I expect that fear would be even higher today. Although Fannie Lou Hammer, a sharecropper and civil rights activist, was talking about racism in the U.S., her statement at the Democratic National Convention in 1964 is applicable here concerning gun violence: "Nobody is free [safe] until everybody is free [safe]." Nobody is safe from violence until everybody is safe.

The U.S. is a violent society, especially compared to our Western European counterparts. Statistics can be easily found online. School and other mass shootings are in the news so often that television stations could almost reserve a portion of their regular programming, much like they do for the weather and traffic reports, for shooting reports. I've had conservative Christian friends and family tell me that the easy accessibility of guns is not the problem and is an area on which we should just agree to disagree.

Agreeing to disagree is what we do for which restaurant has the best sushi or the most generous happy hour. Agreeing to disagree does not work for societal epidemics like gun violence. Dismissing easy gun access as a mere disagreement in perspective is a cop-out. Every time there is a mass shooting, someone will report from the political right that it's the mental illnesses that people have that are the problem, and those people with mental illness get hold of guns. This, frankly, makes the point that guns are too easily accessible. Of course, mental health services in our communities are underfunded. But mental illness is not the primary problem, at least the way the political right means it. I believe that we in the U.S. have a collective mental health problem, which is responsible. We are more concerned with our narcissistic rights, as well as an antiquated interpretation of the Second Amendment than finding solutions to this rapidly growing societal epidemic, a parent's and grandparent's worst nightmare. Times change, and laws change in response. When the U.S. Constitution was written, it was still legal for a man to beat his wife, as long as the stick he used to beat her with was smaller than the base of his thumb—"the rule of thumb." By 1920, it was illegal in all states of the U.S. for a man to beat his wife. (This had become law in Great Britain in 1871.) The Equal Pay Act made it illegal to pay a woman less than a man for essentially the same job. These are examples of how laws change with the times as they change. A while ago, I told a guns rights friend of mine that I would be more impressed with his side of the argument if organizations like the NRA would recognize their responsibility in this issue and would at least support and encourage research for this societal ill.

However, in our country to the contrary, powerful gun rights lobbies like the NRA have pushed successfully since the 1990s to decrease the amount of research on gun violence and deaths. What is up with that? They're afraid that the more we understand this societal ill, gun sales and profits might very well change. This is capitalism run amok. The goal is not to take away guns but to find ways to turn the tide on gun deaths. Similarly, the research on Motor Vehicle Accidents aims not to eliminate cars or driver's licenses, but to enhance car safety and refine associated laws. Research is recognized as necessary to understand how societal epidemics can be slowed and even stopped. Why would we not want the same for gun-related violence and deaths?

Homelessness: As I mentioned at the beginning of the book, a thread that began at seven years old as a result of my Grandfather Willard Palin's example is part of the reason I rarely pass someone needing a handout without giving them something. In our cars, we carry twenty-dollar gift certificates to a local grocery store chain in our part of Colorado. This way, we always have something to give. A couple of the frequent routes I take when I ride my recumbent trike go by places that homeless men sometimes are sitting either to get out of the cold or out of the direct sun. I almost always carry some cash when I ride in case I need to stop and get a snack. Plus, I may come upon a homeless person. A while ago, when riding, I noticed a man sitting at a table that was under a shelter. So I turned off the trail toward the shelter. As I got closer, it was clear he was probably homeless. He was sitting by an old bike with his pack and sleeping bag. I rolled up to the table and said hi. He had a disheveled but kind and gentle look about him. I asked him if he was homeless. With a meek and kindly smile, he said, "Pretty much." I asked him if he needed some money, and he said that he did. I told him I didn't have much but would give him what I had, which was ten dollars. He thanked me. As I rode away, I felt neither happiness at having given him something, nor relief, but instead was gripped by a combination of sadness and anger. Sadness about his situation, and that I didn't have more to give him. Anger over the epidemic of homelessness in our country, and the fact that what I did wouldn't go very far at all to help his situation. I don't know what the solutions are, but we don't seem to have any proper solutions on the horizon. The only time this is in the news is when a city government is doing "a sweep" of homeless camps to clear the homeless out of an area. As we sweep this issue under the rug, so to speak, it's clear to me that we are guilty of spending enormous amounts of money on many other things that have no lasting value, and far too little on things that do count for eternity. One example is military defense: the U.S. spends more than nine other countries combined: China, Russia, India, Saudi Arabia, the United Kingdom, Germany, France, South Korea, and Japan. I'm not suggesting we shouldn't be prepared to defend our-selves. But that level of extremism is careless and irresponsible when we have the number of homeless people that we have, and the thousands of people who do not have adequate health care.

Religious Freedom is one of the five pillars of the First Amendment. Along with free speech, religious freedom is an important essential hall-mark of the U.S. Constitution. I was in high school when the Supreme Court decided, based on the prohibition of state-sponsored religion, that school-sponsored Bible reading and, by association, prayer were banned. Contrary to the views of the adult conversations expressed in and around my conservative religious community, I thought this was a fair and positive thing. I believed and still do that prayer and Bible Study should be the responsibility of the family and church, synagogue, and mosque. I don't want a person who has radically different beliefs from mine instructing my grandchildren on how to pray, what to pray for, or which religious text should be followed.

My oldest son and his family are Muslim. His extended family and many friends are Muslim and Jewish. We have found, without exception, a gracious acceptance of us and our Christian faith. It is disappointing that when this has come up in conversation with other Christians, we have not always found the same level of acceptance and warmth. This lack of reciprocal acceptance bears a striking resemblance to what I frequently encountered in my doctoral studies. My fellow university colleagues, students, and faculty were always accepting of my faith when I could articulate the role my faith played in my life. Yet, this was often not the case when my church community was aware of my chosen profession in psychology. On several occasions, fellow church members, including professional ministers, would say something like, ". . . you weren't a Christian when you decided to go into Psychology, right?" The implication was that it was too bad that I must have already invested in a profession that was "not Christian." This is one reason I have been drawn gradually to more liberal and more accepting faith communities and found Episcopalianism to be a good fit—personally, professionally, and socially. On occasion, when I hear someone spout off about how bad the Muslims are, or, as I have heard from students, how Catholics are not really Christian, I always ask them how many people they know well who hold these beliefs. How many friends do they have that are Muslim or Buddhist? Their answer is always "none." This suggests that they hold opinions that may have no more depth than cocktail-party or coffee-fellowship chatter between Sunday School and the morning service. Or worse, they've adopted the opinions and views from others, often from a leader, without thinking critically about the opinions they've accepted. Those kinds of strong second-hand opinions, without firsthand knowledge, seem not that far afield from a cult.

So when I hear and see organizations proclaim that the U.S. has forsaken its Christian roots, I bristle. The U.S.'s foundations are in religious freedom, among many other freedoms and liberties.

Veterans Issues:

I am obviously sensitized to issues concerning U. S. veterans for several reasons. My personal experiences in the Vietnam War are a significant reason. My oldest son, Scott, was an Army physician who served tours in Kosovo and Baghdad, Iraq. Additionally, my years working directly with veterans in the VA system in the 1970s and when I returned to clinical work in 2010 in Colorado Springs with active duty combat soldiers. I have taken opportunities to support veterans and programs focused on veterans' issues. A few years ago, I was privileged to testify before sub-committees in the Colorado Senate and House of Representatives on the unique needs of Veterans involved in the legal systems, as well as the need for a national suicide hotline, which is easier to remember 988.

Sources and Reading List

BUDDHISM:

Drew, Rose, (2011) *Buddhist and Christian: Dual Belonging.* Routledge, Publishers

Easwaran, Eknath, (1987) *The Upanishads: A Classic of Indian Spirituality,* Nigiri Press

Hanh, Thich Nhat (1995) *Living Buddha Living Christ,* Riverhead Books

Knitter, Paul, (2013) *Without Buddha I Could Not Be a Christian,* Oneworld Academic Publishers

Knitter, Paul & Roger Haight *Jesus and Buddha: Friends in Conversation,* Orbis Publishers

Salguero, C. Pierce (2022) *Buddhish: A Guide to the 20 most important Buddhist ideas for the curious and skeptical.* Beacon Press, Boston

de Silva, Padmasiri (1991) *An Introduction to Buddhist Psychology,* Macmillan Academic & Professional Publishers

Tarrant, John (2008) *Bring me the rhinoceros: and other zen koans that will save your life.* Shambala Press, Boulder, CO

Trungpa, Chogoyam (2015) *Shambahala: The Sacred Path of the Warrior,* Shambahala Publications, Boulder, CO

Wright, Robert, (2017) *Why Buddhism is True.* Simon & Schuster

RELIGION:

Bawer, Bruce, (1997) *Stealing Jesus: How Fundamentalism Betrays Christianity*, Three Rivers Press

Elie, Paul, (2003) *TheLife You Save Might Be Your Own: An American Pilgrimage*, Farrar, Straus, & Giroux, New Your

Finley, James (2017) *Merton's Palace of Nowhere, 40th Anniversary Edition*, Ave Maria Press, Norte Dame, Indiana

Forest, Jim (2011) *All is Grace: Biography of Dorthy Day*, Orbis Books

Hienz, Donald, (2020) *Life After Trump: Achieving a New Social Gospel*, Cascade Books, Eugene OR

Mayfield, D. L. (2020) *Myth of the American Dream*, InterVarsity Press

Mayfield, D. L. (2022) *Unruly Saint - Dorthy Day*, Broadleaf Books

Merton, Thomas, (1948) *Seven Story Mountain*, Harcourt Brace

Rohr, Richard, (2003) *Everything Belongs: The Gift of Contemplative Prayer*, The Crossroad Publishing Company

Rohr, Richard, (2011) *Falling Upward: A Spirituality for the Two Halves of Life*, Jossey-Bass

Rohr, Richard, (2016) *Divine Dance: The Trinity and Your Transformation*, Whitaker House, Publishing

Ord, Thomas J. & Ord, Alexa (Editors) (2023) *Why the Church of the Nazarene Should be Fully LGBTQ+ Affirming*, Sacra Sage Press

Pugh, Jeffery, (2008) *Religionless Christianity: Dietrich Bonhoeffer in Troubled Times*, MPG Press, Great Briitan

Pugh, Jeffery, (2022) *Cages: A Tale of Insurrection*, Resource Publications, Eugene, OR

RACISM

Benedict, Marie & Christopher- Murray, Victoria, (2021) *Personal Librarian*, Berkley

Brooks, Geraldine, (2022), Horse, Viking Press

Jennings, Willie James (2010) The Christian Imagination: Theology & Origins of Race, Yale Press

Morrison, Toni, (Editor) (1998) *James Baldwin Collected Essays*, The Library of America

Stevenson, Bryan, (2014) *Just Mercy: A Story of Justice and Redemption*, Spiegel Grau

Whitehead, Colson, (2016) *The Underground Railroad*, Random House

Whitehead, Colson, (2019) *The Nickel Boys*, Anchor Books

Acknowledgements

Thanks to Dr. Anthony Moore, EdD, for allowing me to tell part of his story of his experiences as a student, professor. Thank you Tony.

More appreciation than words can express to Joyce, my loving wife of 60 years. She has willingly read, reread, and reread the several iterations of this project. Joyce, you know how much I love you.

About the Author

Doug Henning lives with his wife Joyce of 60 years in Parker, Colorado. The couple has two sons and six grandchildren. He is a Vietnam War veteran. He has a Bachelor's Degree in Corrective Therapy and a Master's Degree in Psychology from Pacific Lutheran University in Tacoma, Washington. His PhD is from Oregon State University. Doug completed an Internship in Sexual Dysfunction in the Adult Development program at the University of Washington in Seattle, did a Clinical Fellowship in Rehabilitation Psychology at The Rehabilitation Institute in Kansas City, Missouri, and completed a graduate Certificate in Cross-Cultural Ministry at Nazarene Theological Seminary in Kansas City, Missouri. He has held professional licenses to Practice Psychology in Washington State, Kansas, Missouri, and Colorado.